Labour, Policy, and Ideology in East Asian Creative Industries

This book addresses some of the questions that have been brought to light by the varied experiences of culture industry workers and consumer publics across East Asia over the past decade.

For over twenty years, the creative industries have been seen as the engine driving global economic transformation, as a way out of the dilemmas of de-industrialization, and as key to the projection of national soft power. The chapters in this book cover the former 'Tiger Economies' of South Korea, Taiwan, and Singapore, as well as Japan and China, and focus on a number of different industries – cinema, television, graphic design, fashion, and literature. The authors include sociologists, anthropologists, and cultural studies scholars who approach the topics of creative work, government policy, and entrepreneurial strategy from a variety of perspectives. The chapters examine the varied political, economic, and social structures that influence the development of creative industries within the region and reveal how the careers of creative industry workers in different cities and different industries can vary. They also show how the development of the creative industries can affect many aspects of society, including city planning, policing, democratic politics, and ethnic and national identities.

This book was originally published as a special issue of *Culture, Theory and Critique.*

Teri Silvio is an Associate Research Fellow at the Institute of Ethnology at Academia Sinica, Taiwan. She is the author of *Puppets, Gods, and Brands: Theorizing the Age of Animation from Taiwan* (2019).

Lily H. Chumley is Associate Professor of Media, Culture and Communication at New York University, USA. She is the author of *Creativity Class: Art School and Culture Work in Postsocialist China* (2016).

Labour, Policy, and Ideology in East Asian Creative Industries

Edited by
Teri Silvio and Lily H. Chumley

Routledge
Taylor & Francis Group
LONDON AND NEW YORK

First published 2020
by Routledge
2 Park Square, Milton Park, Abingdon, Oxon, OX14 4RN

and by Routledge
52 Vanderbilt Avenue, New York, NY 10017

Routledge is an imprint of the Taylor & Francis Group, an informa business

British Library Cataloguing in Publication Data
A catalogue record for this book is available from the British Library

ISBN13: 978-0-367-33302-7

Typeset in Minion Pro
by Newgen Publishing UK

Publisher's Note
The publisher accepts responsibility for any inconsistencies that may have arisen during the conversion of this book from journal articles to book chapters, namely the inclusion of journal terminology.

Disclaimer
Every effort has been made to contact copyright holders for their permission to reprint material in this book. The publishers would be grateful to hear from any copyright holder who is not here acknowledged and will undertake to rectify any errors or omissions in future editions of this book.

Contents

Citation Information

The chapters in this book were originally published in *Culture, Theory and Critique*, volume 59, issue 2 (May 2018). When citing this material, please use the original page numbering for each article, as follows:

Chapter 1
After creativity: labour, policy, and ideology in East Asian creative industries
Teri Silvio
Culture, Theory and Critique, volume 59, issue 2 (May 2018) pp. 75–80

Chapter 2
Korea's blacklist scandal: governmentality, culture, and creativity
Ju Oak Kim
Culture, Theory and Critique, volume 59, issue 2 (May 2018) pp. 81–93

Chapter 3
Cool governance: Japan's ubiquitous society, surveillance, and creative industries
Kukhee Choo
Culture, Theory and Critique, volume 59, issue 2 (May 2018) pp. 94–118

Chapter 4
Nation branding in contemporary Taiwan: a grassroots perspective
Adina Simona Zemanek
Culture, Theory and Critique, volume 59, issue 2 (May 2018) pp. 119–138

Chapter 5
Representing creative labour and identity in Singaporean graphic novels: Sonny Liew and Troy Chin
Teri Silvio
Culture, Theory and Critique, volume 59, issue 2 (May 2018) pp. 139–157

Chapter 6

The 'diaspora advantage' of Pauline Chan (1956–): from multicultural filmmaker to cultural broker
Audrey Yue
Culture, Theory and Critique, volume 59, issue 2 (May 2018) pp. 158–177

Chapter 7

The paradoxes of creativity in Guangzhou, China's wholesale market for fast fashion
Nellie Chu
Culture, Theory and Critique, volume 59, issue 2 (May 2018) pp. 178–192

Notes on Contributors

Kukhee Choo is Assistant Professor of Comparative Culture in the Faculty of Liberal Arts at Sophia University, Japan. Her research interests are in film and media studies, cultural studies, body and surveillance, postcolonialism, and nationalism.

Nellie Chu is Assistant Professor of Anthropology at Duke Kunshan University, China. Her current research focuses on global supply chains in fashion and the transnational role of migrant entrepreneurs.

Ju Oak Kim is Assistant Professor in the Department of Psychology and Communication at Texas A&M International University, USA. She studies globalization, culture industries, and production culture with a particular focus on East Asia.

Teri Silvio is an Associate Research Fellow at the Institute of Ethnology at Academia Sinica, Taiwan. She has conducted ethnographic research and published on gender and sexuality, fandoms, theatre, puppetry, animation, and design in Taiwan, Hong Kong, China, and Southeast Asia.

Audrey Yue is Professor in Media, Culture, and Critical Theory in the Department of Communications and New Media at the National University of Singapore. Her research covers the fields of Sinophone media cultures, cultural policy and development, and queer Asian studies.

Adina Simona Zemanek is Lecturer in Asia Pacific Studies at the University of Central Lancashire, UK. She currently teaches modules in East Asian philosophy, political changes and social movements in the Asia Pacific, and research methods.

1 Introduction: After creativity: labour, policy, and ideology in East Asian creative industries

Teri Silvio

For over 20 years, the creative industries have been seen as the engine driving global economic transformation, a way out of the dilemmas of de-industrialization, and as key to the projection of national 'soft power' (Nye 1990), that is, non-military geopolitical influence. Some of the industries often placed in this category have histories of a century or more (e.g., cinema, advertising), while some are much newer (e.g., software programming), but the category itself, and the policies around it, are transforming them all.

The term 'creative industries' (along with related terms like 'creative economy', 'creative class' and 'creative cities') emerged in the UK and US from the 1990s through the early 2000s, and by the mid-2000s had been translated and taken up by governments throughout the world, along with new government agencies, public-private partnerships, policies, infrastructure projects and educational programmes aimed at developing national creative industries. Definitions of the creative industries, practices through which creativity is supposedly manifested, and policies designed to encourage creativity have diversified with the globalisation of the discourse. As Kong et al. (2006) discovered, governments in Asia consulted American and European creative economy gurus such as Richard Florida and John Howkins, but each one adapted their terms and suggestions in different ways. South Korea, for example, made massive investments in infrastructure and support for the cinema and music industries, which many credit for the global success of the Korean Wave. The earlier, and continuing, success of Japanese media products, in contrast, has occurred with relatively little government support.

After more than a decade, we can see that in East Asia, as in the US and Europe, the implementation of policies to develop creative industries and creative cities have had some unanticipated results. These range from the opening up of a space for openly LGBT-owned and operated businesses to flourish in Singapore, where colonial anti-sodomy laws still exist (Yue 2007), to work in design, advertising, and architecture being seen as such a reliable pathway from the working to the middle class in the People's Republic of China that parents now force their children to spend years arduously preparing for hyper-competitive art school admission tests (Chumley 2016).

This issue of *Culture, Theory and Critique* addresses some of the questions that have been brought to light by the varied experiences of culture industry workers and consumer publics across East Asia over the past decade. The papers cover the former 'tiger economies' of South Korea, Taiwan, and Singapore, as well as Japan and the PRC, and one paper looks at the organisation of media co-productions among China, Vietnam, Hong Kong and Australia. They focus on aesthetic labour in a number of different industries – cinema, television, graphic design, fashion and literature, as well as government policy and business strategy. Read together, these papers show how diverse the political, economic and social structures are that influence the development of creative industries within the region, and how different the conditions for production and consumption of creative industry products may be, both between different countries and cities, and for different industries.

The papers here draw on a wide range of academic disciplines, including anthropology, sociology, cultural studies, literary criticism and art history. They are in dialogue with the body of inter-disciplinary work on the creative industries that has emerged over the past two decades, with research based on the situation in North America and Europe, and with research within East Asia. One of our purposes in bringing these papers together is to go beyond the goal of provincialising or expanding 'Western theory', although of course the papers do, in different ways, try to achieve that. Like last year's issue on Queer Asia as Critique (*Culture, Theory and Critique* vol. 58, issue 2, ed. Howard Chiang and Alvin Wong), we aim to use 'Asia as Method' (Chen 2010). We want to show not only how conditions in different East Asian contexts challenge influential theories of creativity and its relationship to the global economy, but also how insights that arise from studying and comparing creative industries and creative work in those sites can lead to new theories of the current global condition that can be productively applied across contemporary cultures. Here I want to outline a few themes that draw the papers in this issue into dialogue with each other.

Creative industries and governmentality

One of Richard Florida's most influential propositions in his 2002 book, *The Rise of the Creative Class*, was that the development of a 'creative class' of workers requires the creation of environments that attract innovative, risk-taking people. The cities in the US that attract a high concentration of creative workers and creative businesses, he argued, are those which encourage diversity and openness, including a vibrant experimental arts scene. The correlation between tolerance and diversity and the creative industries has been challenged by the success of new creative industries in countries like the PRC and Singapore, where governments strictly regulate many aspects of citizens' lives, and artists are regularly censored.[1] Several papers in this issue attempt to take a more nuanced look at the relationship between government surveillance and the creative industries by looking beyond the question of how artists negotiate with censors to the larger context of relations among the creative industries, government regulation, and the public sphere.

Ju Oak Kim's paper looks at this question most directly, by exploring one of the many scandals that led to the candlelight protests that brought down the administration of Park Geun-Hye. Like the three previous presidents of South Korea, Park strongly promoted the creative industries, and encouraged the population to take pride in the global success of the Korean Wave. When it was revealed that Park had kept a blacklist of artists unfriendly to

[1]The connection has also been challenged by developments in the US since the publication of Florida's book by growing class inequality and segregation in cities like San Francisco even as the software and other creative industries flourish (Florida 2016).

her administration, and worked to exclude them from government and private support, many ordinary South Koreans were outraged. Kim uses Foucault's distinction between sovereignty and governmentality to argue that Korean artists' and consumers' emotional investment in the creative industries is deeply tied to ideas of creative work as both actualisation of authentic national and personal identity and as a public good.

The global success of Japanese media products, unlike Korean ones, has occurred largely without government aid, but the government has been eager to use that success to promote national pride and international tourism, often without understanding these products' subcultural appeal (Daliot-Bul 2009; Miller 2011; Choo 2012). Kukhee Choo's paper examines another, more indirect way, in which the government of Tokyo has been inspired by creative industry products. Choo analyses a popular 2007 anime, *Coil – A Circle of Children*, a futuristic fantasy in which an augmented reality environment is accessed through special glasses and policed by armed surveillance robots indifferent to human life. She argues that the anime prefigures the city government's installation of ubiquitous surveillance cameras in Akihabara, the neighbourhood which is the centre of anime/manga fan subculture. The mixed utopian and dystopian aspects of the anime's fantasy world mirror the ambivalent stance of the Tokyo government towards Akihabara and its subcultures, simultaneously seeking to promote them as a tourist attractions and purify and police them.

Teri Silvio's paper, on how two Singaporean graphic novelists represent creative labour and labour conditions, also moves beyond the well-researched issue of how Singaporean artists negotiate government censorship to focus on how these artists redefine creativity both in tension with and incorporating the ideology of profit-oriented pragmatism that the government has promoted since the 1960s.

Nation branding by and for whom?

Another theme that runs through several of the papers here is national branding. Over the past decades, creating a brand image for the nation has increasingly been seen as critical to projecting soft power overseas and instilling national pride domestically, and developing creative industries and creative cities is seen as critical to the nation branding process. Adina Zemanek's paper addresses this issue directly, looking at the motivations and aesthetics of three Taiwanese graphic designers doing 'grassroots' nation branding. Zemanek's paper is in dialogue with a growing body of research, much of it done in Eastern Europe (Graan 2016; Kaneva 2012), which compares the nation and city branding strategies of governments with those of local residents, much of which finds that bureaucrats' ideas of what will attract foreigners often clashes with what citizens actually identify with. Zemanek finds that while Taiwan's official tourism bureaus and city planners focus on displaying traditional high culture and globally generic infrastructure projects (such as high end shopping malls), grassroots creative workers prefer to create products that reflect the heterogeneity of contemporary urban life, choosing parodic and bricolage aesthetics over the serious and purified. One aspect of Taiwanese design that Zemanek notes is its emphasis on the everyday, on the nostalgic rather than the antique or hyper-modern. In this, independent Taiwanese designers seem quite similar to those in Hong Kong (Chu 2012; Ling 2012). The papers by Choo, Kim, and Silvio may also be read as addressing the contradictions between bureaucrats' and creative workers' ideas about the fraught relationships among creative industry work, government-led nation branding initiatives, and the affective politics of national identity, about what gets displayed and what gets hidden in different types of creative projects and products.

Entrepreneurial careers and the gig economy

By now a fair amount of research has been done on how the transformation of culture industries into creative industries is changing the conditions and meanings of labour in the arts. Several aspects of labour in the creative industries have been noted by researchers in North America, the UK, and East Asia. These include the spread of precarious, contract-to-contract freelance labour from the fine arts to related fields (design, architecture) and beyond; the increasing lack of separation between work and play, amateur and professional; the increasingly utilitarian value assigned to artistic labour and competition based on narrowing criteria; and the increasing class and geographical separation between creative workers who design products and the supposedly 'uncreative' workers who manufacture them (for example, see McRobbie 1998; Ross 2003, 2009; Hesmondhalgh 2007; Hartley 2008; Pang 2012; Win 2014).

In Japan, ethnographic work has been done on the more secure but still overworked and underpaid labour of animation workers and on the flows of aesthetic elements and personnel between fandoms and professional manga publishers and animation studios (Condry 2013). In China, creative industries research has focused on the way that international intellectual property law and Chinese workers draw different boundaries between what is 'original' and what is a 'copy' (Pang 2012; Wong 2013), and on the way that creative workers are trained and their professional self-styling (Chumley 2016).

In this volume, the papers by Zemanek and Silvio give some examples of individual creative workers' motivations and how they manage their careers in the marginal gig economies of Taiwan and Singapore. These designers and graphic novelists see their work as intimately tied to projects of constructing new national identities. Audrey Yue's paper looks at the career of Pauline Chan, a 'Vietnam-born, Hong Kong-educated, US-trained, Australian film director, television actress, and media producer', who has accessed what Yue calls her 'diaspora advantage' to create new cooperative projects and enterprises between Australia, Vietnam, Hong Kong, and the PRC. Yue challenges the usual national frame in which creative industries are studied, and draws attention to the way that individual creative workers are negotiating not only with national creative industry policies but also with changing international relations and immigration policies.

The artists studied in these three papers are among the most privileged of creative workers, who have not only achieved a relatively rare degree of economic success within the gig economy, but also national and even international recognition. Nellie Chu's paper provides an important counterbalance to these papers, looking at workers within China's creative economy who must struggle to be recognised as 'creative' at all. Her ethnography of Guangzhou's Xi Fang Hang wholesale fast fashion market focuses on how the discourse of creativity works as an arena of contestation between migrant entrepreneurs and local building managers. Designating clothing designs and how they are selected and displayed as either original or copied becomes a weapon in struggles over the distribution of the enormous risks of an unpredictable and constantly changing global market.

Chu's insight here resonates throughout this issue. Creativity has been defined as an industrial resource, a quality of individuals, groups, or things, and a universal human potential. But as these papers read together show, it might be best to treat it as a contested and floating signifier. The creative industries, creative economy and creative class are likewise not categories that can be deduced from empirical research, but concepts that are constructed and reconstructed through their deployment (in both words and deeds). Creativity is a concept evolving through dialogues among differently positioned actors within and between industries, governments and publics.

Disclosure statement

No potential conflict of interest was reported by the author.

References

Chen, Kuan-hsing. 2010. *Asia as Method: Toward Deimperialization*. Durham, NC: Duke University Press.

Choo, Kukhee. 2012. 'Nationalizing "Cool": Japan's Global Promotion of the Content Industry'. In Nissim Otmazgin and Eyal Ben-Ari (eds), *Popular Culture and the State in East and Southeast Asia*. London: Routledge, 85–105.

Chu, Stephen Yiu-wai. 2012. 'Brand Hong Kong: Asia's World City as Method?' In Chan Kwok-bun (ed), *Hybrid Hong Kong*. London and New York: Routledge, 95–107.

Chumley, Lily. 2016. *Creativity Class: Art School and Culture Work in Postsocialist China*. Princeton, NJ: Princeton University Press.

Condry, Ian. 2013. *The Soul of Anime: Collaborative Creativity and Japan's Media Success Story*. Durham, NC: Duke University Press.

Daliot-Bul, Miki. 2009. 'Japan Brand Strategy: The Taming of "Cool Japan" and the Challenges of Cultural Planning in the Postmodern Age'. *Social Science Japan Journal* 12:2, 247–266.

Florida, Richard. 2002. *The Rise of the Creative Class*. New York: Basic Books.

Florida, Richard. 2016. 'Hip, Cool and Unaffordable: The Double-Edged Sword of Big City Living'. *Alternativesjournal.ca* 42:2, 42–48.

Graan, Andrew. 2016. 'The Nation Brand Regime: Nation Branding and the Semiotic Regimentation of Public Communication in Contemporary Macedonia'. *Signs and Society* 4:S1, S70–S105.

Hartley, John. 2008. 'From the Consciousness Industry to the Creative Industries: Consumer-Created Content, Social Network Markets, and the Growth of Knowledge'. In Jennifer Holt and Alisa Perren (eds), *Media Industries: History, Theory and Methods*. Oxford: Blackwell, 232–244.

Hesmondhalgh, David. 2007. 'Creative Labour as a Basis for a Critique of Creative Industries Policy'. In Geert Lovink and Ned Rossiter (eds), *MyCreativity Reader: A Critique of Creative Industries*. Amsterdam: Institute of Network Cultures, 59–68.

Kaneva, Nadia (ed). 2012. *Branding Post-Communist Nations: Marketizing National Identities in the "New" Europe*. New York and London: Routledge.

Kong, Lily, Gibson, Chris, Khoo, Louisa-May and Semple, Anne-Louise. 2006. 'Knowledges of the Creative Economy: Towards a Relational Geography of Diffusion and Adaptation in Asia'. *Asia Pacific Viewpoint* 47:2, 173–194.

Ling, Wessie. 2012. 'From "Made in Hong Kong" to "Designed in Hong Kong": Searching for an Identity in Fashion.' In Chan Kwok-bun (ed), *Hybrid Hong Kong*. London and New York: Routledge, 153–170.

McRobbie, Angela. 1998. *British Fashion Design: Rag Trade or Image Industry?* London: Routledge.

Miller, Laura. 2011. 'Cute Masquerade and the Pimping of Japan'. *International Journal of Japanese Sociology* 20, 18–29.

Nye, Joseph. 1990. 'Soft Power'. *Foreign Policy* 80, 153–171.

Pang, Laikwan. 2012. *Creativity and its Discontents: China's Creative Industries and Intellectual Property Rights Offenses*. Durham, NC: Duke University Press.

Ross, Andrew. 2003. *No-Collar: The Humane Workplace and its Hidden Costs*. Philadelphia: Temple University Press.

Ross, Andrew. 2009. *Nice Work if You Can Get it: Life and Labor in Precarious Times*. New York City, NY: NYU Press.

Win, Thet Shein. 2014. 'Marketing the Entrepreneurial Artist in the Innovation Age: Aesthetic Labor, Artistic Subjectivity, and the Creative Industries'. *Anthropology of Work Review* XXXV:1, 2–13.

Wong, Winnie Won Yin. 2013. *Van Gogh on Demand: China and the Readymade*. Chicago: University of Chicago Press.

Yue, Audrey. 2007. 'Creative Queer Singapore: The Illiberal Pragmatics of Cultural Production'. *Gay and Lesbian Issues and Psychology Review* 3:3, 149–160.

2 Korea's blacklist scandal: governmentality, culture, and creativity

Ju Oak Kim

ABSTRACT
This essay focuses on the relationship between culture and governance, exploring how the practice of government has invoked conflicts and crises in the Korean culture industries. The Park Geun-Hye regime used culture as a central engine to boost Korea's national economy by adopting the new slogan, 'Creative Korea', to embody the country's national values within the international community. However, the regime's constant emphasis on creative economies came under attack when it was discovered that the Ministry of Culture and Tourism abused its authority by censuring 9,473 artists who were critical of the regime. Through an analysis of journalistic interviews with artists, critics and cultural practitioners, this paper examines how the relationships of governmentality, culture and creativity have been negotiated in the process of regime change. In addition, this paper explores how the Korean Wave phenomenon – the transnational expansion of Korean popular culture – during the past two decades has reshaped the society's perception of the governor–governed relationship within the cultural sphere.

The Korean government has acknowledged the importance of culture in economic development, in which the Korean Wave has expanded the exportation of Korean cultural content and has highlighted Korea's national image within the global community. Enrichment of the culture industries has thus become one of the Korean government's primary considerations in its policymaking process. This policy stance was initially identified in the early 1990s when the Kim Young-Sam regime adopted globalisation as a national agenda to survive in the global capitalist system. Successive governments have implemented various policies to strengthen Korea's cultural power in the global market; for example, the Kim Dae-Jung administration developed an institutional framework to sponsor the arts, media and culture industries. In addition, this administration established several governmental agencies, including the Korean Broadcasting Commission in 2000 and the Korea Creative Content Agency in 2001 (Kim 2012: 48). In the new millennium era, two presidents – Rho, Moo-Hyun and Lee, Myung-Bak – paid attention to the added value of the culture industries, although they took action in different ways. The Rho administration heavily invested in training top-level human resources talent and producing creative content to become a cultural powerhouse in the Asian region (Kim 2012:

50–51). On the other hand, the Lee administration's policy stance on the culture industries claimed to advocate 'creative pragmatism', and implemented a select concentration strategy to strengthen the global competitiveness of specific products and services (Won 2014: 221).

Former president Park, Geun-Hye planned to take one step further to display the country's potential as a rising Mecca of the global culture industry. During her inauguration, Park proposed three key phrases – economic revival, happiness of the people and a flourishing culture – as the regime's vision (Park 2013). She specifically highlighted the power of culture, saying that the Korean Wave is welcomed all around the world with great affection; such a sentiment has instilled abiding pride in all Koreans (Park 2013). She then declared the creative economy as the country's major growth engine, which could be developed through the convergence of scientific technology, industry and culture. Her speech further indicated that the regime would legitimise neoliberal strategies of governing the culture industries through an upsurge of national sentiment (Park 2013).

Whereas the Korean government highlighted its active involvement in expanding Korean popular culture, some critics and practitioners have argued that the experience of producing transnationally appealing popular content has indeed helped Korean cultural actors to decolonise themselves in the global cultural market (Kang 2011; Kim 2016; Lee 2017c). The country's leading music producers – Hyun-Seok Yang, the president of YG Entertainment; and Si-Hyuk Bang, a music producer of BigHit Entertainment – stated that the transborder expansion of Korean pop music enlightened them to see the quality and value of their works differently (K.-H Lee 2011; Chang 2018). Furthermore, Si-Hyuk Bang, who produced BTS, one of the most popular boy bands in the world, claimed that the success of the group was attributable to an accumulation of Korean pop producers and artists' creativity rather than the group's exclusive property (Chang 2018). His argument is helpful in discussing the impact of the Korean Wave in two ways: on one hand, the collective, harmonious and evolutionary creativity of the Korean culture industries has found ways to challenge the US/European-dominated cultural sphere. On the other hand, this local form of creativity indicates that the Korean Wave has not only changed the international audience's perception of Korean popular culture but has also reshaped Korean cultural practitioners' understanding of the self.

It seems certain that the Korean Wave has justified the government's intervention in the culture industries; moreover, it has renewed society's perception of cultural creativity. In this context, this essay calls attention to the Park regime's blacklist scandal that raises fundamental and reflexive questions regarding the relationship between governmentality, culture, and creativity in Korean society. How has neoliberalism shifted the relationship between the government and the culture industries in society? What kinds of tactics did the Korean government employ in order to enrich creative practices and services? Why did the Park regime's blacklist incite resistance not only from listed artists and practitioners but also from the general public? This essay attempts to focus on Korea's corruption scandal through a discussion of governmentality and culture which has mainly been applied to Western societies. Furthermore, this essay attempts to bring the interplay of social systems and individuals' psychological factors in the practice of creativity to the fore of Korean Wave scholarship.

Governmentality and culture: the Korean context

Governmentality studies, developed by Foucault and his colleagues, have provided a fresh and powerful approach to reframing the relation of political power and society (Bratich *et al.* 2003). Foucault initially proposed this analytical tool of political philosophy, defining government as 'conduct of conduct', which refers to a form of practice aiming at managing the practice of people (see Gordon 1991: 2). Foucault further clarified that government mainly concerns relations among individuals involving a form of control or management, relations within social groups, and relations involving the exercise of political power (Gordon 1991: 2–3). Citing Guillaume de la Perriere's definition of government as 'the right disposition of things, arranged so as to lead to a convenient end', Foucault (1991: 93) tried to distinguish government from sovereignty. Whereas sovereignty legitimises the ruler's exercise of power – regardless of its ends – by enforcing the public's obedience to the law, under governmentality, the government should find 'a right manner of disposing things' to ensure everyone the greatest comfort (Foucault 1991: 95). These objectives of government can be obtained through the employment of tactics rather than laws (Foucault 1991: 95). In this light, he underscored the importance of the processes that the government uses to direct, utilise and manage tactics, as well as the ruler's knowledge concerning things that he or she should do to improve 'the welfare of the population' (Foucault 1991: 100). According to Gordon (1991), Foucault further suggests that the practice of government should be aligned with its distinctive form of rationality. Foucault's conception of governmentality, referring to 'a way or system of thinking about the nature of the practice of government' is insightful in examining how governmental strategies can be 'practicable both to its practitioners and to those upon whom it [is] practised' (see Gordon 1991: 3).

This Foucauldian approach is somewhat useful for comprehending how neoliberalism has influenced Korean regimes to reshape the rationality of government in managing the culture industries during the past decades. By the end of the 1980s, popular culture was an object of state control, which the government employed to disseminate the authoritative regime's ideologies (Kim and Jin 2016; H. Lee 2013: 189). These authoritarian regimes – Park, Chung-Hee and Chun, Doo-Hwan – treated the culture industries as an apparatus of national modernisation and instrumentalised cultural content to inspire the national public (L. Lee 2017b). The transformation of policy stance was identified in the 1990s when the Korean Wave penetrated the East Asian region (Jin 2012; Kim and Jin 2016; Kwon and Kim 2014; H. Lee 2013). The Korean government then regarded popular culture as an industry and prioritised 'the internationalization of Korean culture' in the policymaking process (H. Lee 2013: 189). Kim and Jin (2016) highlighted the country's distinctive deployment of neoliberalism in the cultural sectors. In their view, the Korean government set economic development as its prioritised objective and maintained its position as 'a major stakeholder' in the culture industries (Kim and Jin 2016: 5528). Kwon and Kim (2013: 521–22), on the other hand, considered the democratisation of the political system as a determining point that shifted the objectives of cultural policy from censorship and political control to economic enhancement. Since then, the Korean government has implemented various policies to develop industry infrastructures and innovative cultural products (Kwon and Kim 2014: 434).

Some critical cultural scholars, however, assert that it is necessary to critically assess how the country's neoliberal strategies have constructed the complex and hierarchical relationship between the government and the culture industries (Cho 2011; K. Lee 2008; Kim 2016). These critics point out that this approach perpetuates extensive control of the government over the culture industry and exaggerates the economic benefit of cultural expansion (Cho 2011; K. Lee 2008). Relatedly, they claim that by looking at the Korean Wave as 'a symbol of Korean cultural excellence and competence' (Cho 2011: 385) or as the embodiment of creative practices through the exportation of cultural content (K. Lee 2008: 182), the Korean government has maintained its policy stance either in promoting the nation's image (Cho 2011), or in supporting arts and cultures within the context of market assets (K. Lee 2008). These scholars have expressed their concerns regarding the social atmosphere in which both cultural-nationalistic and neoliberal capitalist approaches legitimise the Korean government's selective support of the culture industry and intensify the hierarchical relationship between the government and the culture industry (Heo 2017; Kim 2016). This essay attempts to extend these critical lines of thought on the role of government in the practice of creativity, examining the social impact of the Park regime's blacklist in Korean society. Furthermore, this study seeks to open up the discussion of the Korean Wave as a form of collective creativity, moving forward from its current focus on policy studies.

The interplay of cultural policy and creativity

The process that neoliberalism has unleashed in the operation of governmental policies in the culture industries began with the government's changed perspective on culture. According to Jin-Ryong Yoo, the former Minister of Culture and Tourism, the year 1990 marked an important change in policymaking within the Korean culture industries, in which the Roh Tae-Woo government defined culture as an objective to be achieved in conducting governmental affairs rather as a promotional tool to enhance public relations (Shin *et al.* 2013: 50). In that year, the Roh regime established the Ministry of Culture to enrich the arts and culture through political action. Yoo further claimed that this kind of social change was possibly the result of actions of the Korean public, who had sharply criticised the country's underestimation of the arts and culture during the Park Chung-Hee era (Shin *et al.* 2013: 50). Yoo's argument supports the view that the Korean public has aptly recognised the political and economic power of the arts and culture while experiencing political democratisation and neoliberalisation era (Shin *et al.* 2013).

Since then, the country has developed its specificity in governing culture by introducing a variety of state-driven sponsorships in the fields of the arts and culture. Yoo's claim that public officials should pursue diversity rather than competitiveness in the process of policy enforcement helps us grasp the objectives of government support programmes (Shin, Kim and Lee 2013: 53). He furthered his argument by saying that the Ministry of Culture, Sports and Tourism should concentrate on diminishing social inequalities with respect to the enjoyment of cultural life; in the policymaking process, therefore, preference should be given to creators who had talent, but came from impoverished circumstances (Shin, Kim, and Lee 2013: 53). In fact, the Korean Film Council and the Korean Creative Content Agency often instituted government-funded production programmes, giving preferable consideration to independent filmmakers and content producers (Korean Film Council n.d.; J. Park 2017).

The nature and direction of cultural policy have been transformed during the past decade, in which the presidents ordered governmental institutions to employ economic and industrial logic to policy enforcement (Kwon and Kim 2014; Won 2014). In particular, the Lee Myung-Bak government (2008–2013) made it a priority to sustain the Korean Wave 'by subsidising the participation of Korean firms in international events' (Kwon and Kim 2013: 526). That transformation was somewhat accomplished when the former regimes applied neoliberal thoughts to boosting the exportation of cultural products. The Lee regime concentrated on hosting numerous culture industry forums and conventions, increasing cultural offices in major cities around the world, and holding Korean Wave-related pop concerts and media events (Kwon and Kim 2013: 526). The Korean Wave as the regime's priority in policy enactment allowed public officials to support cultural sectors based on what could be popular in the global market (Kim 2012; Won 2014). This policy stance is often faced with critiques from civilian groups and creative practitioners because of their belief that different and experimental ideas and voices should hardly be chosen by government-affiliated institutions. In these capitalist-centred circumstances, underprivileged artist groups had fewer opportunities to become beneficiaries of the government's support programmes (Shin *et al.* 2013: 59).

As shown in the history of policy development, the government actively decided to take advantage of and further encourage the exportation of Korean popular products. Relatedly, the Korean Wave has opened up the implementation of governmental practices in the culture industries. However, the Korean government's way of thinking about the culture industries has resulted in the commoditisation of popular culture; it has also increased inequality among cultural producers regarding the economic conditions of their creative practices. Therefore, the Korean government's neoliberal approach to culture and creativity, legitimised by the nationalistic and neoliberal promotion of the Korean Wave, has questioned the social and civil benefits of cultural policies among cultural players and members of civil groups (H. Lee 2013).

Governing culture during the Park regime

Former president Park, Geun-Hye emphasised the creative economy as her regime's major objective, legitimising the exercise of power in cultural enhancement. Four years later, however, a political scandal revealed the regime's abuse of power in the culture industries. Choi, Soon-Sil – the former president, Park Geun-Hye's lifelong friend – forced several companies to make donations to culture-related foundations that she had established. Choi's involvement in the government administration displays how the terms 'Korean Wave' and 'creative economy' were used to pursue self-interest rather than to promote cultural diplomacy or the national economy. More significantly, the former president Park, Geun-Hye demanded that government-led institutions and commissions monitor artists and cultural practitioners who were not friendly to the dominating political party. The regime's surveillance on creative individuals confirms that culture became a major governmental apparatus for regulating conduct and for legitimising the use of power necessary to preserve the Park regime.

On 10 October 2016, a member of the National Assembly, Jong-Hwan Do, revealed that the Blue House and the Ministry of Culture, Sports, and Tourism had intervened in the selection of judges who served on the Arts and Culture Commission (Chun 2017: 241).

Do claimed that the former Park regime had controlled governmental officials, artists, and cultural practitioners by monitoring their activities and excluding them from support programmes (Chun 2017). The diary of Young-Han Kim, the former presidential aide, also corroborated the regime's intensive surveillance over leftist artists, writers and practitioners (Cho 2017). According to the diary, Ki-Choon Kim, who worked as the former president Park's chief of staff, instructed staff to 'punish artists who satirised Ms. Park' and to 'make them afraid to challenge the president' during a regular meeting of senior presidential aides in 2014 (Cho 2017).

The revelation of Park's blacklist led cultural critics and researchers to rethink the relationship of culture and governmentality. Chun (2017) juxtaposed the Park regime's artist blacklist with the Nazi book burnings of the early 1930s by pointing out that both events uncovered long-standing and deep-seated social conflicts rather than spontaneous expressions of anger. Since the Korean War, anti-communism and public security have become compelling prisms whereby authoritative governments control their populations and remain in power. The inherent contradiction of the Park regime's vision was also identified in the perspective that cultural enrichment improves citizens' quality of life and disentangles social conflicts (Heo 2017). In Heo's view, cultural enrichment is scarcely realised in the way in which the government selectively supports cultural sectors and pays particular attention to the enlargement of the culture industry. Rather, an improvement of cultural competency is expected within which the government allows freedom of expression, regardless of social and institutional values (Heo 2017). However, the former president had learned from her father, Park Chung-Hee, who had politicised culture during his regime in the 1970s and 1980s. In this context, D.-Y. Lee (2017a: 26–27) argued that in Park, Geun-Hye''s belief system, the blacklist was an appropriate and legitimate operation of government to develop the national culture.[1]

The blacklist scandal fomented multi-layered conflicts in the process of governing culture, not only in the relations between creators and governmental institutions, but also in the relations between governmental institutions involving the exercise of sovereign power. Kim's diary recorded that the regime 'conduct[ed] a "loyalty check" of senior government officials' (Cho 2017). That being said, the governmental officials who enforced supporting programmes in the arts and culture industries found themselves in a difficult situation as the former president ordered the exclusion of leftist artists from governmental grant programmes and mandated that reports on cultural practitioners' activities be communicated to the Blue House. As a result, the former Culture Minister, Jin-Ryong Yoo, and the Vice Culture Minister, Hee-Bum Kim, were forced to leave their positions because their opinions were not compatible with the Park administration on the issue of selectively supporting artists based on their political views (Jung 2016). After the former cultural ministers, Cho, Yoon-Sun and Kim, Jong-Deok, were taken into custody over their involvement in the blacklist scandal, Song, Soo-Keun, the Vice Culture Minister, apologised for the unfairness and discrimination of the operating cultural policies, despite the Ministry's responsibility 'to defend the freedom and creativity of artistic expression' (BBC 2017). In

[1] According to a report of The Economist (2017), government stopped financial support for screening independent films; blockbusters produced by the country's largest media group were the outcome of the regime's pressure, and funding for the Busan Film Festival was no longer available after its screening of a documentary on the Sewol Ferry in 2014. More information is available at https://www.economist.com/news/asia/21715696-supposed-be-liberal-democratic-korea-south-koreas-ministry-culture-accused

his public speech, Song admitted professional negligence in two aspects: governmental officials had adopted a gatekeeping support system for creators, and they had not unearthed the truth for the past years (YTN 2017).

The Korean government has long taken a central position in directing and organising the cultural sectors by government-led sponsorships and regulations that possibly impact the rise and decline of the culture industries. In this structure, creativity can be developed by mutual trust between political and cultural actors (Shin *et al.* 2013: 59). Therefore, the goal of cultural policy is to solidify trustworthy relationships with creators in the arts and culture industries. Yoo's claim that cultural dynamics can be aptly reproduced only when the government, regardless of its political orientation, abides by its own principles, such as fairness, inclusiveness and predictability in the policymaking process reminds us that these principles are key to maintaining a fair and trustworthy relationship between policy-makers and beneficiaries (Shin *et al.* 2013). In this perspective, the blacklist considerably ruined the relation between public officials and creators, and arguably threatened cultural diversity and social equality in the cultural sectors.

Suppressing creativity: exclusion and surveillance

The regime's encompassing approach put numerous artists and cultural players in an extremely awkward position. Some said that their presence on the blacklist had restricted their creative activities. In an interview with the anchor of JTBC's primetime news show, *Newsroom*, Gang-Ho Song, a Korean actor who was blacklisted due to his role in the film, *The Attorney*,[2] confirmed that investors and producers who had engaged in the film underwent hardships (JTBC 2017). In the interview, he also revealed the psychological impact of the blacklist, in which self-censorship had clouded his artistic judgment. Indeed, he hesitated to star in the film *A Taxi Driver* due to the theme of the film possibly making the government uncomfortable[3] (JTBC 2017).

Sung-Dam Hong, the Korean painter, who described Geun-Hye Park as a scarecrow and was later excluded from the Gwangju Biennale – the country's international arts festival – said at an interview with *The New York Times* that the government crushed the creative activities of poor artists in much more direct ways (Cho 2017). As an example, no domestic logistics company was willing to transport his painting when he had been invited by a Berlin arts festival (Cho 2017). Hong assumed that the companies were concerned about government retaliation (Cho 2017). He further claimed that the regime's surveillance often included the family members of the blacklisted artists and creators, assuming that the government had engaged in a tax audit of his wife's clinic (Cho 2017).

The Park regime also controlled the themes of artistic and creative works. Jung (2017b) cited the Sewol Ferry tragedy, which occurred in April 2014, as a determining point when many artists tried to respond to social issues. In his view, some artists who were mostly left-wing at that time, participated in criticising the government; as a result, most of them were under secret state surveillance (H. Jung 2017b).[4] The film director, Joon-Ho

[2]The film, *The Attorney* (2014) involves the former President Moo-Hyun Roh's life and political biography.
[3]The film, *A Taxi Driver* (2017) is based on the historical events of the Gwangju Democratisation Movement.
[4]The Sewol documentary, *Diving Bell*, became a hot-button issue during the 2014 Busan International Film Festival. This regionally renowned festival experienced a considerable budget cut due to the denied state funding after screening the film (Jung 2017: n.p.)

Bong, stated the following in a media conference during the 2017 Cannes International Film Festival that: 'It was such a nightmarish few years that left many South Korean artists deeply traumatised' (H. Jung 2017b). Although Bong's international reputation insulated him from the State's surveillance, he became outspoken in calling social attention to other artists who had been severely threatened concerning their creative activities due to their exclusion from governmental support (H. Jung 2017b).

Blacklisted artists and creators' testimonies raise the question of how political and economic conditions interact with an individual's psychological factors of creativity. Cognitive factors and personal characteristics have initially occupied the discussion of creativity, highlighting the psychology-centred aspects of creativity, including 'motivation, personality, values, and problem solving and problem finding orientation' (Rudowicz 2003: 274). Some scholars, however, called attention to the impact of the system – social rules, customs, and norms – on individuals' creativity to answer questions regarding how 'the existing knowledge, rules, standards and tradition' shape the nature and direction of creative expression and practices (Rudowicz 2003: 274). In this light, some scholars expanded the definition of culture from the construct of a society's traditions, values, beliefs and rules, to a reflection of political, economic and technological conditions. This system-centred approach to creativity somewhat facilitates the process of recognising the influence of political conditions in creative practices (Ludwig 1992: see Rudowicz 2003: 275).

At a certain level, the exclusion of financial support has caused Korean artists and cultural practitioners to have fewer opportunities in the production and circulation of their creative products and practices. Moreover, the recognition of being under surveillance has made it difficult for these artists to further their aesthetic and creative performances without self-censorship. The blacklist scandal thus echoes Chumley's (2016: 8) claim that creativity is shaped by 'a quality of mind' rather than by 'a routinized form of knowledge.' As she notes, if creativity can be 'encouraged' (Chumley 2016: 9), the government's responsibility is to produce creative subjects through the establishment of the mutually constructive governor–governed relationship in the process of policy enforcement and through the protection of the values of individuals' creative thoughts and performances. In this context, the Park regime failed to negotiate between neoliberal thoughts on the practice of creativity and her authoritative approach to governing culture.

Creative practice as political subjectification

The regime's surveillance engendered resistance from artists and cultural practitioners. After a press conference criticising the Park regime's cultural policy and censorship on 4 November 2016, numerous artists and cultural activists staged a rally by camping at Gwanghwamun Square. A cultural activist claimed that the establishment of an encampment and an arts action committee, unleashed by the blacklist scandal, has prompted the discussion of culture and governance in three aspects: (1) setting anti-censorship as a social agenda; (2) showing the encampment as a new type of commons; and (3) proposing new ways of cultural imagination (W. Lee 2017d: 129–137). It is notable that numerous artists and creators joined in solidarity to oppose the regime's way of governing culture. Such collective resistance against the iniquity of governmental practice through the organisation of public forums and artistic performances has become an important and powerful trigger in identifying the blacklist as one of the major issues that destroyed the legitimacy of the Park regime.

Blacklisted artists and creators have played an important role in the formation of collective resistance against the Park regime. Their reactions are not new because the Korean public has witnessed how Korean pop artists and media practitioners have secured their subjectivities for more than almost half a century, negotiating with media institutions and the government's censorship. Showered by foreign popular culture, some Korean musicians, such as Kim, Minki and Han, Daesoo, expressed a spirit of resistance against the authoritative administrations during the 1970s and 1980s (S. Kim 2017). Seo Tai-Ji and Boys, who led to the modernisation and westernisation of Korean pop music in the early 1990s, fought a battle against the government's review system, by releasing his song 'Sidae Yugam' without lyrics (S. Kim 2017). A Korean boy group, BTS also released a song 'Spring Day' in 2017, recalling the victims of Sewol Ferry. A series of examples suggests that Korean artists have attempted to 'form [their] identities and subjectivities through an attachment to the games of truth about [themselves] and the world' (Bratich *et al.* 2003: 9).

Sooner or later, the square became a common area where millions of citizens held candlelight protests to demand that the president step down. These nationwide rallies remind us that culture is often associated with 'modes of political subjectification' (Bratich *et al.* 2003: 8). The hardship that artists, celebrities and creators had experienced due to the blacklist gave the national public an indication as to how self-government intersects with political government, how they are related to members of society, and what kinds of obligations are imposed on them in the operation of a democratic system (Dean 1999). An article in the *New York Times* also provided the rationale behind the society-wide rallies against the Park, Geun-Hye regime's politically biased cultural actions. In Cho's (2017) view, Korean citizens' rage was considerably derived from their memories of intensive censorship and oppression against artists and creators under the Park, Chung-Hee regime. For Korean citizens, the political and economic exploitation of the arts and culture signified a return to the age of dictatorship (Cho 2017).

Another point to mention here is that there was the distinctive gap between the regime and the protesters in understanding the relationship between governmentality and culture. Whereas the regime tried to revitalise the role of culture as a propaganda tool, the protesters expected neoliberal governmentality pertaining to self-development and free expression in the expansion of the Korean Wave. In this regard, Korean citizens could not accept the inclusion of some artists and creators on the blacklist who have shown extraordinary ability in their fields, such as Han, Kang, the 2016 winner of the Man Booker International Prize; Park, Chan-Wook, winner of the Grand Prix at the 2014 Cannes Film Festival; and Nah, Young-Seok, a television producer of the reality show format, *Better Late Than Never* – the Korean reality show format to be remade by a US major network. These cultural actors have contributed not only to increasing the outflow of Korean popular culture, but also to deconstructing a western-centred perspective of creativity, either by obtaining international acclaim from or by proposing a format of cultural products within western societies. Given that the legacy of the Korean Wave has taught the general public that the phenomenon is driven by those who established the forms and standards of local/national creativity, the inclusion of these artists' names on the blacklist not only failed to rationalise regime's objective 'the internationalization of

Korean culture' (H. Lee 2013: 189) but also warned the public regarding the tendency of the practice of government 'towards a form of political sovereignty' (Gordon 1991: 3).

In March 2017, the country's constitutional court removed president, Park, Geun-Hye from power after millions of Korean protesters, from teenage students to elderly citizens, participated in collective, harmonious and peaceful street demonstrations. These nationwide political rallies can be viewed an important example of how individuals have constructed their subjectivity of being solidified citizens, resisting against the iniquity of being exploited by political power. It is also notable that, despite the gravity of the issue, Korean citizens have shaped protests as moments of festivity. A CNN report (2016) claimed that these calm but joyful rallies reflect the characteristics of Korean pop music. In a similar way, a Korean poet viewed the candlelight rallies as the public's artistic achievements (H. Jung 2017a). With that being said, the way that the Korean public has expressed its objections against power reflects what it thought about governmentality in the fields of arts and cultures.

Conclusion

Neoliberalism, under the new forms of globalisation and governmentality, has promoted the intervention of government in the Korean culture industries. Hence, since the 1990s, the expansion of the Korean Wave has become one of the major objectives in the policy-making process. In this context, policy studies have spotlighted the Korean government's financial and diplomatic support in the production and distribution of cultural content (H. Lee 2013; Jin 2016; Kwon and Kim 2014). Relatedly, Korean journalism has aggressively provided major coverage of Korean pop music, television dramas, online gaming, and reality television which have penetrated multiple cities throughout the world (K. Lee 2008). The discourse of the Korean Wave has thus focused more on the state-driven strategy of enriching cultural activities. As a result, the salience of cultural policy in enhancing the national economy by boosting the culture industries has dominated the national discourse (H. Lee 2013; Jin 2016; Kwon and Kim 2014).

This societal environment deeply affected the beginning and end of the Park, Geun-Hye regime. Former president Park declared her devotion to cultural enrichment and a creative economy in her inauguration speech to legitimise the expansion of political intervention within the culture industries. She promised to support creative activities to 'foster a new cultural renaissance and a culture that transcends ethnicity and languages, overcomes ideologies and customs, and contributes to the peaceful development of humanity' (Park 2013). However, when it was publicised that her support had excluded left-wing artists and cultural practitioners, Korean citizens considered such action as an unacceptable threat to the nation's political system and removed the regime from power with street demonstrations.

The blacklist scandal highlights some assumptions regarding the power of government against cultural practitioners implicit in the fields of the arts and culture in Korean society. First, mutual trust between government officials and creative actors concerning fairness and inclusiveness in policy enforcement is deeply involved in the practice of creativity. Second, state surveillance crystallised fundamental changes in the country's cultural policy, which failed to implement cultural enrichment. The political exploitation of cultural production had ruined 'the formation of new subjectivities' (Mitcheson 2012: 59) which were essential in the creation of different and alternative ideas and practices. Finally, my claim that the Korean Wave is not merely a transfer of Korean cultural values and ideas to other societies but also a product of Korean cultural practitioners' collective creativity provides a different approach to understanding the corruption scandal. As mentioned in the earlier section, the renewed understanding of self can be applied not only to cultural actors but also to Korean citizens; they have thus considered the blacklist as an anachronistic and regressive action of government in the era of the Korean Wave.

Acknowledgements

I would like to express my sincere gratitude to two anonymous reviewers whose comments clarified my argument. I would also like to thank Teri Silvio for giving me insightful comments, Lily Chumley for inviting me to this special issue, and Christopher C. Barnes for helping me out during the publishing process.

Disclosure statement

No potential conflict of interest was reported by the author.

Funding

This project received no external funding.

References

BBC. 2017. 'South Korea Ministry Apologises over Artists' Blacklist'. *BBC News*. 23 January. Available online at http://www.bbc.com/news/world-asia-38716305 (accessed 31 August 2017).

Bratich, Jack Z., Jeremy Packer and Cameron McCarthy. (eds). 2003. *Foucault, Cultural Studies, and Governmentality*. Albany, NY: State University of New York Press.

Chang, Yun-Jung. 2018. 'Bang-si-hyeog "Je-i Je-sam-ui Bang-tan-so-nyeon-dan-eun Eobs-da"' [Bang, Si-Hyuk, "I won't produce the second and third versions of BTS"] [In Korean]. 1 January. Available online at http://www.ajunews.com/view/20171220105247117 (accessed 3 January 2018).

Cho, Younghan. 2011. 'Desperately Seeking East Asia Admist the Popularity of South Korean Pop Culture in Asia'. *Cultural Studies* 25:3, 383–404.

Cho, Sang-Hun. 2017. 'South Korea's Blacklist of Artists Adds to Outrage Over Presidential Scandal'. *The New York Times*, 12 January. Available online at https://www.nytimes.com/2017/01/12/world/asia/south-korea-president-park-blacklist-artists.html?mcubz=3 (accessed 31 August 31 2017).

Chumley, Lily Hope. 2016. *Creativity Class: Art School and Culture Work in Postsocialist China*. Princeton, NJ: Princeton University Press.

Chun, Sung-Won. 2017. 'Bag-geun-hye Jeong-bu-ui "Beul-laeg-li-seu-teu" Sa-tae-leul Ba-la-bo-myeo' [On the Park Geun-Hye Regime's 'Blacklist' Scandal]. *Citizen & the World* 30, 239–252. Available online at http://www.dbpia.co.kr/Article/NODE07203616

CNN. 2016. 'South Korean Protestors Find Inspiration in K-pop'. *CNN.* 13 November. Available online at http://www.cnn.com/videos/world/2016/11/13/south-korea-k-pop-protest-orig.cnn/video/playlists/south-korean-president-park/ (accessed 31 August 2017).

Dean, Mitchell. 1999. *Governmentality: Power and Rule in Modern Society.* London: Sage.

Foucault, Michel. 1991. 'Governmentality'. In Graham Burchell, Colin Gordon and Peter Miller (eds), *The Foucault Effect: Studies in Governmentality with Two Lectures by and an Interview with Michel Foucault.* Chicago, IL: University of Chicago Press, 87–104.

Gordon, Colin. 1991. 'Governmental Rationality: An Introduction'. In Graham Burchell, Colin Gordon and Peter Miller (eds), *The Foucault Effect: Studies in Governmentality.* Chicago, IL: University of Chicago Press, 1–52.

Heo, Min. 2017. 'Beul-laeg-li-seu-teu-wa Seo-myeong-ui Jeong-chi' [The Politics of Blacklist and Signing]. *The History for the Future* 66: 300–309. Available online at http://www.dbpia.co.kr/Article/NODE07122666

Jang, Hoon. 2017. *A Taxi Driver.* Korea: The Lamp.

Jin, Dal Yong. 2012. 'Cultural Studies in Korea's Contemporary Films Under Neoliberal Globalization'. *Media, Culture & Society* 28:1, 5–23.

Jin, Dal Yong. 2016. *New Korean Wave: Transnational Cultural Power in the Age of Social Media.* Chicago, IL: University of Illnois Press.

JTBC. 2017. 'Yeong-hwa-bae-u Song-gang-ho' [Actor, Kang-Ho Song]. *JTBC News,* 25 May. Available online at https://www.youtube.com/watch?v=OvzUYpecA-k (accessed 5 January 2018).

Jung, Min-Ho. 2016. 'Former Top Presidential Aide's Home Raided'. *The Korea Times.* 26 December. Available online at http://www.koreatimes.co.kr/www/news/nation/2016/12/116_220874.html (accessed 24 February 2018).

Jung, Hee-Sang. 2017a. 'Bag-geun-hye-neun Yeog-sa-ui Beul-laeg-li-seu-teu-e Deung-jae-doel Geos' [Park, Geun-Hye Will Be Recorded in History]. *Sisain.* 2 February. Available online at http://www.sisain.co.kr/?mod=news&act=articleView&idxno=28260 (accessed 19 February 2018).

Jung, Ha-Won. 2017b. 'From Blacklist to Blockbuster: Bong Joon-ho Bounces Back at Cannes'. *Asia Times.* 18 May. Available online at http://www.atimes.com/article/blacklist-blockbuster-bong-joon-ho-bounces-back-cannes/ (accessed 31 August 2017).

Kang, Myung-Suk. 2011. 'E-seu-em-i Yu-leob-e Tong-ha-neun I-yu-neun Tta-lo Iss-da' [There Is Another Reason Why SM Has Penetrated the European Market]. *10Asia.* 21 June. Available online at http://tenasia.hankyung.com/archives/8430 (accessed 2 January 2018).

Kim, Kee Hyun. 2012. 'Mun-hwa-san-eob Jeong-chaeg-ui Byeon-dong-e Gwan-han So-go' [A Study on the Formation and Changes of the Cultural Industry Policies]. *The Journal of Culture Contents* 12: 31–68.

Kim, Ju Oak. 2016. The Korean Wave as a Localizing Process: Nation as a Global Actor in Cultural Production. *Doctoral Dissertation.* Philadelphia, PA: Temple University.

Kim, Sang-Hwa. 2017. 'Seo-tae-ji I-sib-o-ju-nyeon-eu-lo Doe-dol-a-bon Geu Si-jeol Eum-ban Sa-jeon Geom-yeol' [Retelling the History of Record Censorship in Commemoration of Seo Tai-ji's 25th year Anniversary]. *Ohmynews.com.* September 9. Available online at http://star.ohmynews.com/NWS_Web/OhmyStar/at_pg.aspx?CNTN_CD=A0002358384&CMPT_CD=P0010&utm_source=naver&utm_medium=newsearch&utm_campaign=naver_news (accessed 6 February 2018).

Kim, Tae Young and Jin, Dal Yong. 2016. 'Cultural Policy in the Korean Wave: An Analysis of Cultural Diplomacy Embedded in Presidential Speeches'. *International Journal of Communication* 10, 5514–5534.

Korean Film Council. n.d. 'Jin-heung-sa-eob Gae-yo' [An Overview of Supportive Programs]. Available online at http://www.kofic.or.kr/kofic/business/prom/introPromotion.do (accessed 4 January 2018).

Kwon, Seung-Ho and Kim, Joseph. 2013. 'From Censorship to Active Support: The Korean State and Korea's Cultural Industries'. *The Economic and Labour Relations Review* 24: 4, 517–532.

Kwon, Seung-Ho and Kim, Joseph. 2014. 'The Cultural Industry Policies of the Korean Government and the Korean Wave'. *International Journal of Cultural Policy* 20: 4, 422–439.

Lee, Keehyeung. 2008. 'Mapping Out the Cultural Politics of "the Korean Wave" in Contemporary South Korea'. In Chua Beng Huat and Koich Iwabuchi (eds), *East Asian Pop Culture: Analysing the Korean Wave*. Hong Kong: Hong Kong University Press, 175–190.

Lee, Kyung-Hee. 2011. 'Yang-hyeon-seog, Big-baeng, Sin-han-lyu-seu-ta-me-i-keo ... Han-gug-pan Gu-geul-eul Mal-ha-da' [Big Bang/New K-pop Starmaker, Yang, Hyun-Seok Talks About 'the Korean Version of Google]. *Herald Economy*, 26 May. Available online at http://news.heraldcorp.com/view.php?ud=20110525000888&md=20120422140327_BL (accessed 4 January 2018).

Lee, Hye-Kyung. 2013. 'Cultural Policy and the Korean Wave: From National Culture to Transnational Consumerism'. In Youna Kim (ed), *The Korean Wave: Korean Media Go Global*. Oxon, OX: Routledge, 185–198.

Lee, Dong-Yeon. 2017a. 'Beul-laeg-li-seu-teu-wa Yu-sin-ui Jong-mal' [The End of the Blacklist and the Yusin Regime], *Culture & Science* 89: 26–52.

Lee, La-Young. 2017b. 'Beul-laeg-li-seu-teu, Tong-je-wa Eog-ab-ui Yeog-sa' [The Blacklist, Korea's Cultural History of Suppression and Control]. *Pressian.com*. 11 December. Available online at http://www.pressian.com/news/article.html?no=178865&utm_source=naver&utm_medium=search (accessed 31 January 2018).

Lee, Sang-Heun. 2017c. 'Nyu-yog Gang-ta myu-ji-keol "Ke-i-pab" Jag-gog-ga Hel-len Bag' [Helen Park, Who Produced a Musical, 'KPOP' in New York]. *Weekly Chosun*. 23 October. Available online at http://weekly.chosun.com/client/news/viw.asp?nNewsNumb=002479100025&ctcd=C09 (accessed 2 January 2018).

Lee, Sang-Ho and Ahn, Hae-ryong. 2014. *Diving Bell: The Truth Shall Not Sink with Sewol*. Korea: Asia Press-Cine Port.

Lee, Won-Jae. 2017d. 'Beul-laeg-li-seu-teu Ye-sul-geom-yeol-e Jeo-hang-ha-neun Ye-sul-un-dong-ui Sil-cheon-gwa Jeon-mang' [Cultural Movements against the Blacklist and Censorship]. *Culture Science*, 89: 127–144. Available online at http://www.dbpia.co.kr/Article/NODE07132585

Ludwig, Arnold. 1992. 'Culture and Creativity'. *American Journal of Psychotherapy* 46:3, 454–469.

Mitcheson, Katrina. 2012. 'Foucault's Technologies of the Self: Between Control and Creativity'. *Journal of the British Society for Phenomenology* 43: 1, 59–75.

Park, Geun-Hye. 2013. 'Bag-geun-hye Dae-tong-lyeong Chwi-im-sa' [President Park Geun-Hye's Inauguration Speech]. *KTV*. 25 February. Available online at http://www.ktv.go.kr/content/view?content_id=456685 (accessed 17 June 2017).

Park, Jung-Kyu. 2017. 'Han-kon-jin, 50eog-won Gyu-mo Bang-song-kon-ten-cheu Dog-lib-je-jag-sa Ji-won Si-jag' [Korean Creative Content Agency Will Spend Five Billion Won in Supporting Independent Production Companies]. *Kwangju Ilbo*, 27 July. Available online at http://www.newsis.com/view/?id=NISX20170727_0000053267&cID=10701&pID=10700 (accessed 4 January 2018).

Rudowicz, Elisabeth. 2003. 'Creativity and Culture: A Two Way Interaction'. *Scandinavian Journal of Educational Research* 47:3, 273–290.

Shin, Dong-Yeop, Eun-Mee Kim, and Joong-sik Lee. 2013. *Chang-jo-seong-ui Won-cheon [The Origin of Creativity]*. Seoul: Gimmyoung-sa.

Won, Do-Yeon. 2014. 'I-myeong-bag Jeong-bu I-hu Mun-hwa-Jeong-chaeg-ui Byeon-hwa-wa Mun-hwa-min-ju-ju-ui-e Dae-han Yeon-gu' [The Characteristics of Lee Myung-Bak Administration's Culture Policy and the Search for the Timely Change]. *Humanities Contents* 32, 219–245.

Yang, Woo-seok. 2014. *The Attorney*. Korea: Withus Film.

YTN. 2017. 'Mun-che-bu, Mun-hwa-ye-sul-gye "Beul-laeg-li-seu-teu" Dae-gug-min Sa-gwa' [The Ministry of Culture, Sports and Tourism Publicly Apologized for the Blacklist Scandal]. 22 January. Available online at https://www.youtube.com/watch?v=uwCS9NtlR3Y (accessed 31 August 2017).

3 Cool governance: Japan's ubiquitous society, surveillance, and creative industries

Kukhee Choo

ABSTRACT
The rapid reform of the Akihabara district of Tokyo during the first decade of the twenty-first century, in conjunction with the Japanese government's policy on the global promotion of *Cool Japan*, has been envisioned under the Japanese government's new direction of becoming a 'ubiquitous society'. From the postwar period when Akihabara became the techno-gadgetry hub of Tokyo, into the twenty-first century where it transforms itself into the Mecca of anime and video games, Akihabara has become the embodiment of national hope and technological future. Noticeably, what also implemented alongside this advance of techno-future is a new form of governance and surveillance. After Katō Tomohiro's murderous rampage in Akihabara in 2008, numerous CCTVs have been installed to secure the neighbourhood from crime and news of this solution became a spectacle in international media. This form of ubiquitous techno-governance integrated as part of everyday life had already been imagined in anime such as *Dennō Koiru* (Coil A Circle of Children), which broadcast on Japan's national broadcast station NHK in 2007. In light of the concerted effort of the Japanese government's promotion of anime to the global consumers seamlessly integrating the urban developmental project of Akihabara, the production of *Dennō Koiru* at that historical juncture presents a pertinent foreshadowing of Japan's 'society of control'. This article will examine the notion of ubiquitous society and surveillance in *Dennō Koiru* and situate its production against the backdrop of Japan's growing techno-governance vis-à-vis its creative industries in the twenty-first century.

Surveillance has become a part of our everyday lives. Jeremy Bentham's vision of the panopticon, analysed by Michele Foucault, has become a lived reality as witnessed in the aftermath of incidents such as Rupert Murdoch's News International admitting in 2011 to phone tapping, the United States National Security Agency (NSA) intercepting private citizens' phone calls exposed by Edward Snowden in 2013, and WikiLeaks revealing in 2017 that the CIA surveils televisions, smartphones and computers. Popular depictions of societies run by governmental surveillance often appear in either dystopian futures under the logic to maintain utopian calm, seen in futuristic science fiction films such as *Gattaca* (1997), *Minority Report* (2002), *Equilibrium* (2002), and *V for Vendetta* (2006), or in conspiracy-thrillers such as *Enemy of the State* (1998), *The Bourne Identity* (2002), *Eagle Eye* (2008), and *Furious 7* (2015) that dramatise the depth of surveillance in the present. In particular the aftermath of the 9/11 attacks has brought forth a global alliance on the war against terror led by the United States, enforcing strict surveillance mechanisms at airports and communication devices and technologies (Lyon 2009, 2004: 143). The duality of Western societies against the terrorists from certain regions in the world has created a pan-global fear, anxiety and heightened awareness of the ever-shifting body of the 'other'. What is striking in this process is the different treatments, or modes of surveillance, that have emerged out of countries such as Japan, which have not experienced international terror attacks on their soils.

Unlike Western countries' heightened security and surveillance to counter both domestic and international terrorism, Japan's recent developments or modes of surveillance are embedded in its futurist vision of ubiquitous society, its promotion of creative industries as well as the ambivalent relationship of these industries with 'internal others' such as the otaku, and their cultural appeal to global consumers. Since 2008, various locales in Japan have begun to install CCTV to ensure safety for its citizens, mostly through private enterprises. However, no other space has created such a national spectacle in its installation of a CCTV system than Akihabara, a neighbourhood on the east side of the city of Tokyo. Akihabara is known as 'Japan's Silicon Valley', which historically contributed to the development of Japan's software industries (Ibata-Arens 2005: 138). Also termed the 'electric city' (*denkigai/dennōgai*), Akihabara is the primary space where 'major electronic companies such as Sony, Panasonic and Hitachi, to name a few, all release their products for consumer testing on the streets' (DiMarco 2004: 45). Utilising the term 'city' when describing the neighbourhood of Akihabara indicates the special positionality placed upon this particular space in terms of marketing and consumer dynamics. What is more, since the turn of the new millennium, Akihabara has also become the locus of the manga, anime and video games industries' vitality, making it into a unique testing ground for varied visions of Japan's techno-futurity, conjured up by both governmental and private sectors, to compete, collide, synthesise and materialise for both domestic and international consumption. Owing to the Japanese government's global promotion of popular culture and creative industries, guided under the banner *Cool Japan* since the mid-2000s, the space of Akihabara has gathered much attention from global consumers of Japanese popular cultures. After the 2008 Akihabara massacre and the subsequent installation of CCTV cameras, the space of Akihabara was further transformed into the harbinger of Japan's society of control where surveillance is seamlessly integrated into the free-flowing imagination of the creative industries and the global consumption of Japanese popular culture. Interestingly, this kind of everyday ubiquitous techno-governance and consumerism had already been envisioned in the anime *Dennō Koiru* (Coil A Circle of Children, 2007), making it an exemplary cultural text for thinking through the entangled desires and fears associated with the Japanese government's embrace of ubiquitous society, surveillance and soft power.

The new vision of Akihabara

Akihabara, which first began as a district where one could purchase radio and television parts in the postwar era of Japan, quickly emerged as the centre of attraction for many foreigners (Senoh 2007: 14–5). What used to be viewed as the techno-gadget district of Akihabara has transformed itself into the Mecca of anime, video games and maid cafes in the twenty-first century – in other words, a special enclave for 'otaku', a Japanese term for 'geeks' – which now attracts many foreign otaku tourists as well (Akiba Keizai Shimbun 2007: 6). Post-2005, Akihabara witnessed a rise of visitors that created what is called '*hokōsha tengoku*' (pedestrian heaven), or 'hokoten', owing to the popular film *Densha Otoko* (2005) and the opening of mega electronic store Yodobashi Camera (geek 2008: 10) (see Figure 1 and 2). As an extension of Akihabara, Tokyo has become the headquarter of Japan's soft power in regards to the shifting socio-economic as well as political landscape of the production and global consumption of anime, manga and video games.

In the early 2000s, the city planned to rebuild Akihabara into a digital media centre by forming intellectual alliances with academic institutions. The Digital Hollywood University was established in 1994, which was sponsored by major corporations in various industries, including Hitachi, Ltd., Uchida Yoko Co., Ltd., TAITO CORP., Kansai Telecasting Corporation, and NAMCO LTD. In 2001, the highly esteemed Keio University established research institutions in Akihabara, turning it into a new geographic hub for partnership between universities and industries. The prestigious University of Tokyo also set up a branch campus in Akihabara to train IT specialists and promote the industry through 'academia tie-ups in research, product development, and test-marketing' (Stefik and Stefik 2004: 205).

With these changes came the new urban development of housing, corporate architectures and train stations. Tsukuba Express was built in 2005, which linked Tokyo to Tsukuba city in Ibaraki Prefecture located 50 km northeast of Tokyo. Tsukuba was a city that underwent an overhaul during the 1960s and was reborn as a 'science city'.

Figure 1. Major electronic store in Akihabara, November 2017 (photo taken by author).

Figure 2. A woman advertising for a maid café in Akihabara, November 2017 (photo taken by author). Faces intentionally blurred to protect subject privacy and identity.

At the heart of the new project was the newly established University of Tsukuba, envisioned to contribute to Japan's leading science and technological innovations. The belated 2005 Tsukuba Express was to accelerate transportation between Tokyo and Tsukuba, and noteworthy is the fact that the main station in Tokyo is located in Akihabara. The existing Akihabara subway and train stations were also refurbished in the mid-2000s, which further accelerated the pace of the ever-changing landscape of Akihabara as a whole.

The population that transited through Akihabara station increased from 120,000–130,000 per day in 2001 to 200,000 in 2005 (Senoh 2007: 20) and television programmes began to broadcast on the changed image of Akihabara. Moreover, the Tokyo Animation Center and The Association of Japanese Animations (AJA) are housed in the newly constructed UDX building, located immediately across from the train station, attracting many anime fans from both Japan and abroad. Foreign visitors to Akihabara also increased from the mid-2000s owing to the global recognition of Japanese popular culture (officially referred to as the 'Content industry'). Subsequently, to the Japanese policy makers, Akihabara became a space that could attract global consumers as well as promote Japan's creative industries abroad.

Governmental promotion of Japanese popular culture

Stemming from the Prime Minister Koizumi Junichirō's 2002 Intellectual Property Act, the Japanese government passed a bill in 2004 to promote the creative industries, consolidated under the title *Content industry*,[1] which at the time covered creative industry media such as manga, anime, video games, film, television and popular music. The key motivation behind the new support of popular culture was the rise of the Western market since the mid-1990s (Choo 2012: 85). Owing to the global popularity of anime series such as *Sailor Moon* (1992), *Pokémon* (1997) and *Spirited Away* (2001), the Japanese government began to focus on promoting the Content industry to international markets. Since there were already waves of Japanese popular culture circulating throughout the Asian markets since the late 1980s (Iwabuchi 2002), the Japanese government's drastic attitude shift towards supporting popular culture in the early 2000s was a clear response to the Western market's rising potential at the time.

The new official promotion has since been referred to as *Cool Japan*, utilising a Western term appealing to the targeted consumers. The Tokyo Metropolitan Government has created various international venues such as media and film festivals where foreign consumers and investors can get direct access to the most up-to-date productions. Many festivals and events have been consolidated under the larger Japan International Contents Festival (COFESTA), offering cohesive presentations and access to Content for both domestic and global consumers and industries. As a result, the city of Tokyo has been transformed into the Mecca of Japanese popular culture and with these changes came increased flows of foreign tourists and capital, as well as various changes in the Content industry business infrastructures and urban landscapes.

Most significant is the government's support toward the anime industry. In the initial stages, the government's promotion focused on the video game industry for its high economic returns. However, after positive reports on attitudinal changes among young Asian consumers of Japanese popular culture towards Japan, government officials strategised Content promotion into 'image promotion', which heavily revolved around the anime industry (Choo 2012: 88). As a result, not only has there been an enormous increase in foreign attraction to anime but the city planning around areas such as Akihabara confirms the government's increased support of the anime industry. Once denied as a 'proper' culture, both manga and anime have now become an industry worthy of support by the Ministry of Economic, Trade and Industry (*Keizaisangyōshō*, METI). In fact, manga was elevated to the status of 'traditional' culture by the Ministry of Education, Culture, Sports, Science and Technology (*Monbukagakushō*, MEXT henceforth) in 2000 (Choo 2012: 86). Following this governmental shift was the new image promotion centring on the district of Akihabara where most of the anime fans and consumers of the Content industry conglomerate.

[1]The 'Content industry' is a special term utilized by the Japanese government. The term embodies a particularity that encompasses a broader notion of various media contents, platforms and infrastructures vis-à-vis *Cool Japan*. Therefore, to be faithful to its Japanese terminology, I have capitalized the term 'Content' throughout this essay.

As the Japanese governmental support of the anime industry propelled anime to become the face of *Cool Japan* in the twenty-first century both internationally and domestically, the cityscape of Akihabara (and to an extent Tokyo at large) has also increasingly become a simulacrum of anime itself. Morikawa Kaichirō analyses how Akihabara has transformed into a 'personapolis' where the subjectivity of the otaku desire has manifested onto the cityscape (Morikawa 2003). One can easily spot a plethora of anime imagery plastered onto the urban cityscape when visiting Akihabara (Figure 3). In other words, the internal fantasies and desires, or what Morikawa asserts as 'hobbies (*shūmi*)', of the

Figure 3. Anime and game images on buildings in Akihabara, November 2017 (photo taken by author). Faces intentionally blurred to protect subject privacy and identity.

otaku consumers have translated into power to alter the external reality. In conjunction with the governmental support of the Content industry, especially anime, the velocity of changes witnessed in Akihabara has been remarkable during the first decade of the twenty-first century. It can be argued that the Japanese government's new policy has not only transformed the Content industry but has also visually and physically shaped the urban spaces in Tokyo. This very notion can be witnessed in the narratives and images of the Content itself, creating an interminable cycle of mutual influence between the imagined Content and the constructed realities.

Ubiquitous network society, surveillance and safe space for otaku

In addition to the promotion of the Content industry and its transformative impact on Akihabara, creating a 'ubiquitous society' has been another major project mapped out by the Japanese government since the turn of the new millennium. The notion of ubiquitous society was first introduced to Japan by engineers in the late 1990s. However, not until the 2003 'e-Japan' strategy planning did Japanese research institutes and government start to utilise the term. The e-Japan project was a plan to layout broadband infrastructure throughout Japan. Developing upon this e-Japan was the new vision of creating 'u-Japan' (ubiquitous Japan) where information network technology and infrastructure would correspond smoothly throughout the entire country. Ever since, the Japanese government has been investing to actualise a ubiquitous network society through the development of ICT (information and communication technology) infrastructure and the promotion of ICT utilisation. By 2007, about 25 per cent of the Japanese population heard and knew about the concept of 'ubiquitous society', which was understood to be 'everywhere or in many places at the same time' (Murakami 2007: 10).

Directly involved in this project were the Ministry of Internal Affairs and Communications (MIAC) and the Ministry of Economy, Trade and Industry (METI). MIAC instigated the Ubiquitous Network Society Strategy Program (UNS) in 2005 and the main goal of this new strategy was to build ubiquitous and faster mobility in telecommunications, ubiquitous platforms, secure networks and safety sensing devices (Murakami 2007: 13). The government's plan has been to solve matters such as the aging population, decreasing child birth, medical problems, unemployment, global environmental issues, etc. through establishing a ubiquitous network society (Murakami 2007: 13). In other words, the ubiquitous digital network society in Japan is understood to preserve human dignity by improving people's daily lives. Although most of the claims for the importance of creating a ubiquitous society have been linked to the notion of service solutions for the aging population, where ubiquitous home appliances, automobiles, sidewalks and housing would benefit the elderly and disabled, benefits for the Content industry has also been noted: 'If there are platforms, terminals and networks, you can do a lot of business, and contents (sic) industries will be the first to use that as well as the ubiquitous electronic industries' (Murakami 2007: 13). It was calculated that if the Content industry could utilise the ubiquitous network, it would then in return benefit the country as the Content industry was one of the 'top five strategic industries of the twenty-first century' that the Japanese government designated (METI Report 2004). Furthermore, the 2006 government planning report on the 'u-Japan' project listed three main points for its development: first, to integrate the communication networks including broadcasting; second, to build Japan's soft power that would increase economic growth and competition; third, to establish a ubiquitous society to ensure safety and security (MIAC u-Japan Development Plan 2006). Here is where the vision of ubiquitous society seamlessly integrates with the development of the Content industry; a nation where both the young (Content consumers) and the old (the aging population) could benefit from a shared network of digital information technology. Yet what is missing in the government's portrayal of technological determination toward a ubiquitous society is the surveillance factor that would follow. Overly positive rhetoric of ubiquitous digital technology controlling every aspect of the urban cityscape and ordinary citizens within that space has created an unrealistic, utopian image of Japan's digital future landscape. Akihabara has been the forerunner of that optimistic vision owing to the booming Content industry. Not only would Akihabara be the leading force behind the digital revolution but it would also attract foreign 'otaku' capital that would bolster Japan's economy. However, that confidence was almost shattered overnight, at least in the minds of the Japanese.

In June 2008, a 25-year old male named Katō Tomohiro was captured after running a truck into the central streets of Akihabara and then randomly stabbing people, killing seven and injuring ten.[2] This incident reminded Japan of the 1989 incident when the pedophilic serial killer Miyazaki Tsutomu was captured. Thousands of pornographic anime tapes of young girls were found in Miyazaki's apartment, creating a wave of social backlash and bias against the otaku communities. When the Akihabara massacre occurred in 2008, concerns that the incident would tarnish the image of Akihabara, and subsequently Japan, which would hinder attracting valuable foreign capital into the Content industry, superseded concerns over Katō as an individual or the possible backlash that the domestic otaku would incur. The aftermath of Katō's rampage saw 16 surveillance cameras installed in the district of Akihabara in January 2010. News media noted that 'The cameras were also installed with hopes that the heightened security would provide a feeling of safety and stave off crime, attracting more people to the area'.[3] However, since Akihabara has long been known to domestic consumers in Japan as a place that attracts specific groups of people – the purported techno-gadget, anime, manga and game otaku – who in general have not posed prominent harm to the public (compared to the more realistic threats caused by organised crime elements, for example), the reasoning behind the city's decision to install surveillance CCTV cameras in Akihabara becomes all the more poignant; the rationale behind establishing Akihabara as a 'safe place' by installing surveillance systems was not only to appeal to the global audiences over the domestic ones but also to fulfil the scheme to create a 'ubiquitous society' that was in line with the Content industry.

As mentioned earlier, the digital ubiquitous network that Japan envisions includes not only daily appliances but also public spaces such as digitally monitored street blocks that may assist electronic wheel chairs for disabled people (Ernst 2004: 213). In such cases, the ubiquitous network system and ubiquitous media converges. Bodily subjectivity is monitored and becomes public data. As Douglas Kellner argues, in a ubiquitous media society, 'there seems to be nothing sacred or immune from media scrutiny, leading to an implosion of private and public life' (2003: 102). Furthermore, the city of Tokyo's attempt to

---

[2]Katō Tomohiro incident has been referred to as the 'Akihabara tōrima jiken' (Akihabara random massacre).
[3]http://www.japantoday.com/category/crime/view/16-security-cameras-installed-on-akihabara-streets, Accessed 6 October 2017.

maintain the image of Japan through Akihabara as a safe environment indicates that the district is under the 'politics of surveillance' (Haggerty and Ericson 2006) where the private space is controlled for the good of the public. Yet, the logic to prevent crime in Akihabara by installing CCTV cameras may not be as effective as anticipated by the government as it becomes a lazy form of control and may rather create further indifference by the public. Nicholas Mirzoeff warns us as follows:

> The ubiquitous surveillance cameras of today's society in no way seek to prevent crime or the breaches of social norms, nor do they claim any moralizing effect on the individual ... [it becomes] simply a well-publicized example of the indifference of contemporary surveillance to the individual. (2006: 342)

Once people register contemporary surveillance as indifferent, they become desensitised to the system as banal every day surroundings.

With the understanding of Japan's intent to create a ubiquitous media-led society in the twenty-first century that integrates with the Content industry, I will next examine the significance of the popular anime series *Dennō Koiru* (Coil A Circle of Children, 2007) that aired on the Japanese national broadcast television station, NHK, in 2007. According to Jeffrey Sconce, over the past 150 years, the cultural imagination in relation to emerging new technologies follows three patterns of narratives: first, narratives of 'disembodiment' where the subject leaves the body through electronic means (whether physically or through imagination); second, narratives of the subject entering a 'sovereign electronic world' that has been created by telecommunications technology; and finally, narratives of anthropomorphised media technology, often depicted through androids/cyborgs (2000: 8–10). Interestingly, *Dennō Koiru* follows all three of these narrative patterns. Sconce further asserts that:

> there are tremendous differences in the actual social, cultural and political "content" of these stories within differing historical and technological contexts ... Tales of paranormal media are important, then, not as timeless expressions of some undying electronic superstition, but as a permeable language in which to express a culture's changing social relationship to a historical sequence of technologies. (2000: 10)

In line with this view, *Dennō Koiru*, I argue, magnifies how Japan's ambitious endeavour to create a ubiquitous society merged with the governmental support of the Content industry during the height of initiating both policies and encapsulates the crux of Japan's technological ambitions, aspirations and anxieties at the historical juncture of its production. NHK being the national television station makes this anime series pertinent in terms of how public media manifest multifaceted desires and fears regarding the future of Japan as a ubiquitous society. Moreover, the storyline becomes a fascinating case study on how globalisation, digital technology and urban spaces have been reconfigured, reimagined, and renegotiated by the creative Content industry and consumer/otaku culture.

Dennō Koiru (Coil A Circle of Children, 2007)

Created by Iso Mitsuo, the 26 episode *Dennō Koiru* (henceforth *Coil*) produced by Madhouse Inc. animation studio aired during the 6:30 pm slot on Saturdays on NHK Educational Broadcast Station (NHK E-Tele) from 12 May to 1 December 2007. The entire series was rebroadcast immediately starting from 8 December 2007. Animations aired

Figure 4. Augmented reality glasses in *Dennō Koiru*. The two female protagonists Yasako (right) and Amasawa (left) get caught up on a larger conspiracy revolving the virtual reality city of Daikoku. ©Mitsuo Iso / Tokuma Shoten – CyberCoil Production Committee.

on NHK E-Tele are considered for younger children, but in the case of *Coil*, with its sophisticated plot structures, the target audience was upper elementary school children and older. *Coil* won the Excellence Award in Animation at the 2007 Japan Media Arts Festival held by the Agency for the Cultural Affairs, a subdivision of the Ministry of Education, Culture, Sports, Science and Technology (MEXT) and also won the Japan SF Grand

Prize in 2008. The narrative of *Coil* revolves around a virtual reality city called Daikoku. The city's name derives from one of Japan's seven lucky gods, *Daikokuten* (great blackness), who came to represent wealth and fortune through its name also resonating with the Japanese term 'great nation' (*Daikoku/Taikoku*).

In Daikoku city, the landscape infrastructure consists of digital data and the Internet that can be accessed through special 'augmented reality' glasses (Figure 4). However, the viewers do not realise that the spaces that the characters reside in are holographic urban spaces until the latter part of the series. Yet, unlike visually limited holograms, the virtual reality in which the characters live is physically accessible. The story focuses on a special group of elementary school children, who constantly live in a shared virtual reality space by wearing their special glasses on a daily basis. The glasses become tools to manipulate the data surrounding their everyday lives. The glasses function as not only to access the Internet, but also as digital weapons (when engaging with other video game players). And the virtual spaces that they enter and control become their own reality.

The main female protagonist Okonogi Yūko, who prefers to be called by her nickname Yasako (written as 'kind child' in *kanji* characters), is a transfer student who moves to the city of Daikoku because of her father's work. Daikoku is also where her grandmother lives. After exploring the neighbourhood, Yasako and her younger sister Kyōko discover mysterious 'black spaces' called 'coil domain' throughout the area, which turn out to be remnants of old data that have not been 'formatted' into the current city space. Yasako's digital bulldog Densuke accidentally gets stuck in one of the black spaces and therefore faces the danger of being formatted and erased by the city's surveillance robots called Satchi (searchmatons) (Figure 5).[4] Satchi do not discriminate at whom they shoot their digital

Figure 5. Satchi machines chasing after Yasako and her pet dog. ©Mitsuo Iso / Tokuma Shoten – Cyber-Coil Production Committee.

[4]A similar autonomous surveillance robot was developed in the United States in 2013 (https://www.nbcnews.com/tech/innovation/hiring-r2d2-protect-your-mall-or-campus-all-6-25-n262796).

Figure 6. Fumie (Left) sends her digital pet Oyaji into the coil domain to rescue Densuke, Yasako's digital pet dog. ©Mitsuo Iso / Tokuma Shoten – CyberCoil Production Committee.

beams, and the only spaces safe from them are the old temples. A passer-by, whose name is Hashimoto Fumie, instructs the two neighbourhood newcomers on how to escape from Satchi. Fumie also opens up cracks in the coil domain, which leads to Densuke's rescue (Figure 6).

Yasako and Fumie become good friends after Yasako transfers to a new school where they become classmates. Most of the children in the class wear their special augmented reality glasses. The children access the Internet, play online games, and do online shopping with their glasses (Figures 7 and 8). Their hands function as gadgets while wearing these glasses; e.g., typing into air in order to access the Internet and spreading their thumb and pinkie finger to use as a phone receiver. The physical body becomes tuned in to the virtual reality spaces. The children's playtime also involves war games, in which each character can instantaneously purchase online digital weaponry (digital beams) or protection shields. The battle scenes resemble those of online role-playing games. Thus, the anime portrays network games becoming integrated into physical reality, similar to the *Pokémon Go* game that the world has witnessed in recent years. Yasako's bespectacled Grandmother, fittingly named Megabaa (a combination of Japanese words for eyeglasses and grandmother), owns a digital data candy shop where one can purchase various shields, data boosters, and antidotes to network viruses created out of 'metatags', which are fragments of digital data. They are portrayed in a manner resembling traditional Japanese/ Chinese talismans (*ofuda*) written on paper (Figure 9). However, these metatags become 'absorbed' into the virtual body and function as digital antivirus programmes.

In Yasako's surroundings, temporal and spatial realities have no boundaries. The blurring of the digital and the physical environment alters the linear notion of space and time. It is later revealed that Yasako's grandmother Megabaa is a legendary hacker whose knowledge of the digital database space surpasses even the city's officials, who built, maintain and surveil Daikoku. Megabaa organises a group called Dennō Coil Investigation

Agency where Yasako's friend Fumie is a member. Yasako also joins in order to figure out the mystery behind the unexplained black spaces.

Figure 7. Children can instantaneously download image files and view them. ©Mitsuo Iso / Tokuma Shoten – CyberCoil Production Committee.

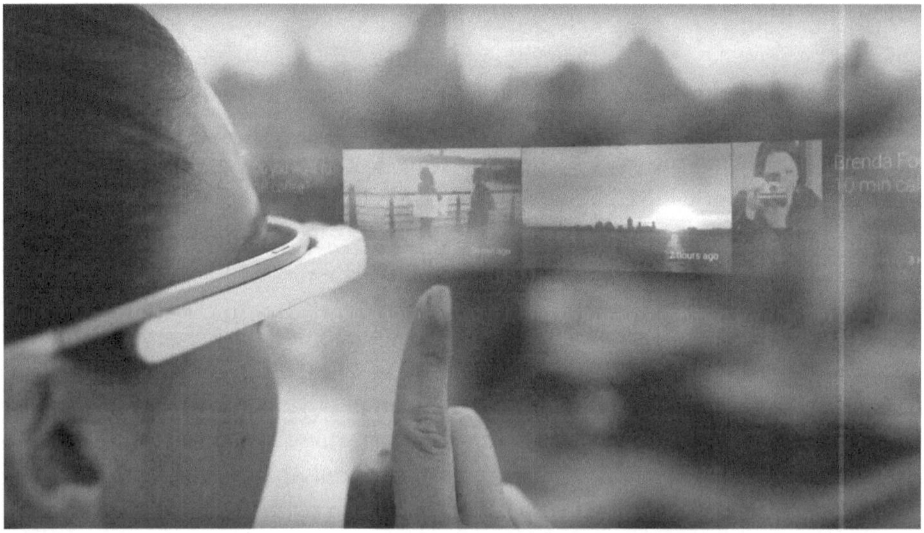

Figure 8. A similar concept is witnessed in Google Glass released in 2013. Courtesy *Google*, https://www.google.com/glass/help/.

After another female student, whose name is coincidentally also Yūko, transfers to Yasako's class, the plot deepens. The new Yūko (whose kanji name is 'brave child') is given a nickname 'Isako' (brave child) by her classmates, but goes by her surname Amasawa. She appears as an indifferent but aggressive person who does not get along

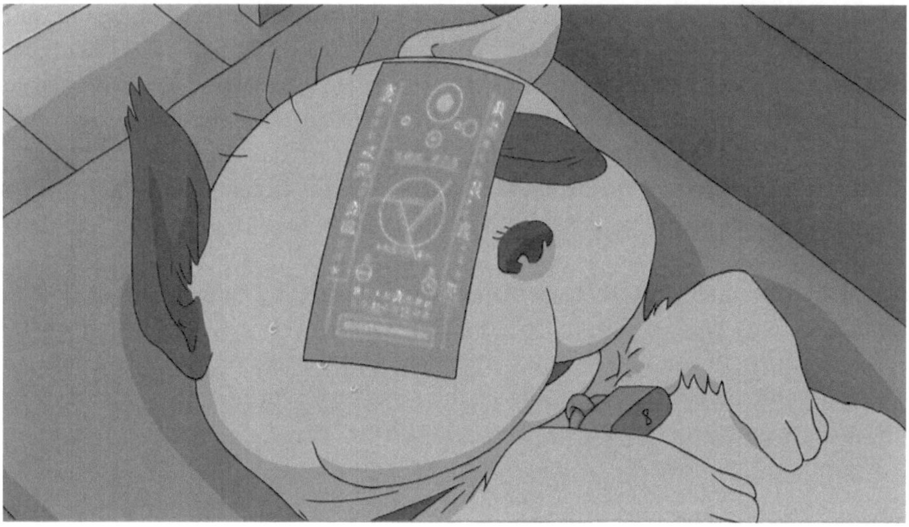

Figure 9. Virtual pet Densuke is being cured by being given a metatag. ©Mitsuo Iso / Tokuma Shoten – CyberCoil Production Committee.

with anybody. As the story unfolds, we encounter a larger conspiracy that the city has been trying to conceal the danger of the newly developed virtual technology, which is responsible for creating entities called 'ghosts'. These 'ghosts' are revealed to be remnants of the left over old data, which could also include the 'ghost' of humans who died while wearing the augmented reality glasses. In fact, Amasawa's brother was part of a digital experiment conducted by the city a few years back. He fell victim to the new technology and is in a coma. In attempts to bring back her brother, whose 'soul' is assumed to be stuck in the old database coil domain space, Amasawa tries to open up a larger portion of the black space. This goes against Daikoku city's policy which is to completely eliminate any existing unformatted space. Amasawa becomes an underground resistance activist against the city's formatting policy. She becomes a fugitive from authorities whilst gathering data boosters in order to upgrade her 'digital' strength. Amasawa uses her classmates as pawns to rapidly gather metatags.

The audience witnesses Yasako's childhood memories and learns how they are linked to Amasawa's comatose brother. Yasako tries to prevent Amasawa from her illegal actions in vain. Amasawa's determination eventually leads to a massive opening of the coil domain, and in the process, both Amasawa and Yasako get stuck in it. Within the old database space, Amasawa and Yasako encounter their old 'ghosts'. Yasako sees her own childhood where she is talking to Amasawa's brother at a shrine, and Amasawa meets Michiko, an urban legend ghost character that is widely known among school children in Daikoku. Later, Amasawa realises that her own grief, anger and hatred are the source of Michiko's creation. When Amasawa finally encounters her brother in the coil domain, she comes to terms with the idea that it is only appropriate to let go of her desire to relive her childhood with her brother. After realising this, Michiko, the manifestation of Amasawa's angst, disappears, and both Amasawa and Yasako return to reality.

In the final episode, we are exposed to the entire city landscape of Daikoku as being that of a virtual reality space witnessed from the children's perspectives while wearing their glasses. The virtual city of Daikoku is projected upon a normal suburban neighbourhood under a different name that one can easily encounter in Japan. The space of Daikoku was produced by the special glasses, but their experiences are visceral and 'real'. If one gets a digital beam attack while in Daikoku, then one's physical body suffers. If the attack is severe enough, then a person can even lose their life. Yasako's digital pet Densuke, which dies in the middle of the series, is not visible to the human eye without wearing the glasses. Nevertheless, Densuke's death deeply affects Yasako, as much as the urban legend of Michiko's existence scares the children. The sentiments resulting from the virtual world profoundly affects the protagonists' realities. The entire series of *Coil* ends with either parents confiscating the children's glasses or the children taking off their glasses voluntarily. In the end, Yasako enjoys walking in nature along with her sister Kyōko, and both see Densuke standing in the middle of a neighbourhood street, even without their augmented reality glasses.

Database, knowledge and anime

Although *Coil* ends on a moralistic and idealistic note, probably due to it being broadcast on NHK, it raises imperative questions about the current state of how digital technology is imagined to intertwine with the everyday lives of the younger generation in Japan, especially in regard to otaku culture. Paul Roquet analyses *Coil* as a narrative that 'presents childhood as a critical period for learning to navigate the interface between the composited self and the augmented environment' and that 'the show presents [augmented reality] athleticism as the *only* option for a successful childhood' (2016: 240–1). Here, the athleticism that Roquet asserts is related to the augmented labour that the children have to physically, intellectually, and emotionally experience (2016: 241). However, I argue that in *Coil*, the Foucauldian notion of power heavily relies on data-based knowledge. Thus, Yasako's grandmother Magebaa becomes the pinnacle of computer knowledge because of her understanding of old computer technology, which has given her a master-like understanding of the entire network society's structure. In the final episode, Yasako's father is also revealed to be a specialist in database network systems, positioning the older generations as more knowledgeable and thus 'powerful'. The same can be said with Yasako's classmates. Whoever has more access to or knowledge of online databases or merchandise, especially during digital warfare, holds power.

According to Azuma Hiroki (2001), Japanese anime and its avid otaku fans have created a space where modes of communication and consumption have been altered into a postmodern 'database-like' structure. The signified are codified into bits and pieces of information that are condensed into the notion of 'moe', a term that summarises an appealing and exciting element in a character. Moe elements do not have a linear history that can add up to the characters' attractiveness. Azuma asserts that the characters themselves become an embodiment of the entire history of anime character development and thus, become transcending figures of the otaku culture. In other words, contemporary anime and its characters are produced with prior creations as stepping stones, only to further blur the boundaries of narratives, visuality and the history of the medium itself. Therefore, the entire genre of anime becomes an agglomeration of postmodern pastiche and stereotypes. Azuma's conceptualisation of otaku 'data-base consumption' and production is epitomised in anime such as *Coil*. For example, character designs in *Coil* resemble those created by the famous auteur anime film maker Miyazaki Hayao. Additionally, Yasako and her sister Kyōko evoke the sister relationship in Miyazaki's anime *My Neighbor Totoro* (1988). However, unlike Miyazaki's emphasis on nature as the primary and redemptive element in his anime films, *Coil* centres on the digital virtual reality and its consumption that is far from the natural environment, which is more in line with the science fiction tradition of Japanese anime.[5]

Evoking the trite bias of techno-Orientalism, Daikoku (which reminds us of the omnipresent god Daikokuten and also echoes the term 'great nation' in Japanese) as a virtual reality city replicates the notion of great economic and technological development that Japan once represented during the Cold War and bubble economy era.[6] According to director Iso, Daikoku city was designed as an amalgam of Hachiōji city (a satellite city about an hour west of Tokyo) and Kanazawa city (a city on the west coast of Japan that boasts rich traditional cultures and architectures) but set in a basin. In the narrative, however, Daikoku city is set as a seaside city near Kanazawa. Owing to not being attacked during World War II, Kanazawa has many traditional shrines and temples intact from the Edo period. This becomes a significant trope throughout the anime series. When data virus-eliminating Satchi machines sweep the cityscape, the only spaces to which the children can safely evacuate are the old temple sites. Here, we can witness the tension among the past, present and the future intertwined with the various narrative structures and pastiched images. Miki Daliot-Bul explains that the Japanese governmental policy to promote popular culture has been heading towards the direction of 'neo-Japonism' where the international promotion of Japanese culture itself may revert back to the age-old self-Orientalisation associated with the promotion of traditional arts in the early twentieth century (2009: 252). The fact that the traditional shrine and temple sites within *Coil* are the only spaces safe from the threat of new computer technology offers interesting insight into how twenty-first century Japan is envisioned and self-Orientalised, especially after the promotion of the Content industry.[7] To present traditional sites in conjunction with the high-tech science fiction elements within the anime narrative echoes the Japanese government's incorporating manga and anime as part of traditional arts. Considering this, the production of *Coil* during the height of the government's global promotion of Content renders it pertinent in the history of Japanese anime as a whole. The desires and anxieties toward technology in *Coil* are represented through the 'cool' lifestyle of the residents in the city of Daikoku, replete with techno-futuristic gadgetry, including the Satchi machines, yet on the other hand, the 'return to nature' at the end of the story exemplifies the laden ambivalence. The appeal of anime, both inside and outside Japan, is often that it depicts Japan as a techno-futuristic country, which is precisely a major attraction of *Coil.* The anime becomes a meme of its own, a database congregate of *Totoro* in futuristic Japan.

As Azuma might see it, database-like knowledge is equivalent to power in *Coil.* The manner in which one consumes the urban space of Akihabara parallels that of how an

---

[5]The ending of *Coil*, however, calls for a return to nature, which is similar to the overarching theme of Miyazaki Hayao's anime films.

[6]Japan became the world's second largest economy by the 1980s but there developed an economic bubble from 1986 when real estate and stock prices became inflated. This bubble burst in 1992 and Japan's economy has suffered since. China surpassed Japan as the second world economic power in 2013.

[7]A similar theme can be witnessed in the anime film *Summer Wars* (2009) by Hosoda Mamoru. In *Summer Wars*, a traditional former samurai clan family living in rural Japan joins forces to fight against a high-tech hacking virus that threatens a global social network platform.

anime otaku retrieves knowledge from the vast anime database history. Akihabara is a space premised upon its previous image of being an electronic city, thus creating invisible conceptual boundaries around it. Thus protected from the outer shields of Tokyo, Akihabara, like the virtual reality basin city Daikoku, is confined to its fantasy realm. Paradoxically, by being excluded as a particular, Akihabara becomes included into the larger imagination of the 'great nation (*daikoku*) Japan', and by its very association with Akihabara, the once alienated otaku subjectivity becomes incorporated into mainstream Japan in this process.

The image of otaku has changed over time. Caught at the crossroads of Japan's vision of ubiquitous society and its promotion of creative industries, the public discourse concerning otaku has shifted dramatically in the new millennium. However, both negative and positive images of otaku and their culture continue to co-exist in Japanese society today. As mentioned earlier, the 2008 installation and spectacle of CCTV surveillance in Akihabara was part of the government's effort to create a ubiquitous society of control in the name of protecting and attracting global otaku consumers.[8] Before that, a discernible social attitude change towards domestic otaku in Japan, mostly imagined as men, came with the popularity of the film *Densha Otoko* (Train Man, 2005). This title first became widely consumed as a novel, based on a live thread on an Internet mega-bulletin board called 2channel, then through a theatrical film, and further branched out into television dramas.[9] Popular variety television shows broadcast experimental programmes that rated the level of 'manliness' among Akihabara otaku men:

> On August 24, 2005, the Fuji television program *Toribia no Izumi* (*Fountain of Trivia*) broadcast an experiment involving 100 *otaku* men who shopped in Akihabara. The experiment was to see how many men would try to rescue a female who was being attacked by a hooligan in the back allies of Akihabara. According to the program, 69 out of the 100 men went out of their way to rescue a female in distress. (Choo 2012: 100)

This episode cannot be an accurate measurement of otaku masculinity, nor should it be viewed as a symptom limited to the space of Akihabara. What can be discerned from this experiment, however, is the fact that one of the most popular Japanese television series of the time conveyed the image of otaku as positive, or becoming 'masculine'. This notion is premised upon the general understanding that otaku male subjectivity is precisely not that of an 'ideal' masculinity, in image that has been delegated to the 'salary men' since the postwar Japan developmental period (Slater & Galbraith 2011). Without this prior knowledge, one would not appreciate the television programme's so-called 'humorous' attempt to measure otaku manliness and therefore, would be excluded from the surprising results that showed almost 70 per cent of otaku men displaying courageous, or conventionally imagined as heteronormative masculine, traits. Once regarded as marginal and socially less-than-desirable, otaku masculinity has not only become mainstream, but it has also come to represent the new-found virility of Japan's neoliberal capitalism in the twenty-first century owing to the government's effort to boost its economy via the creative industries; in other words, the otaku are now responsible for motivating the 12

[8]Galbraith (2010) notes the tension that arose among the Japanese 'real otaku' population against the rise of global popularity of Akihabara.

[9]See Alisa Freedman's '*Train Man* and the Gender Politics of Japanese '*Otaku*' Culture: The Rise of New Media, Nerd Heroes and Consumer Communities', *Intersections: Gender and Sexuality in Asia and the Pacific*, 20 (2009) for details on how *Train Man* became popular in Japan.

billion dollar Content industry. As one Western scholar has observed, 'The losers are now winning, and they are changing Japan along the way' (Leheny 2006: 220). Although the 2008 Akihabara massacre created a temporary backlash against the otaku communities, the overall image of otaku continues to improve and, as discussed above, Akihabara, the Mecca of otaku culture, has become the harbinger of Japan's 'society of control'.

Governance over content bodies

The very confinement to the space of Akihabara has dramatically transformed the otaku subjects into the new face of Japan. When one consumes the space of Akihabara as representing Japan, similar to consuming the entire history of anime through pastiched works of narratives and images, the space of Akihabara, as a result, performs and 'wears' *Cool Japan* for the audience. Although Morikawa (2003) is correct in pointing out that the cityscape of Akihabara has increasingly been shaped by the otaku subjectivities' personal desires, I would argue that it is the national desire of *Cool Japan* that has propelled the rapid transformation of Akihabara into the Mecca of Japanese popular culture as well as the harbinger of a ubiquitous society. Akihabara has become the primary locus for both free-floating global consumerism and governmental surveillance. As Mark Steinberg has argued, early anime characters tie up with merchandise stickers created precursors to contemporary Japan's 'media ubiquity' and 'media mix' (2009: 116). In addition to the long tradition of anime and manga characters as platforms of media ubiquity in Japan, the Japanese government's vision of 'ubiquitous society', as explained earlier, focuses on the control and surveillance of the body through managing data and the physical space, which has been envisioned and critiqued in *Coil*. Gilles Deleuze, by citing Félix Guattari, notes the following:

> The conception of a control mechanism, giving the position of any element with an open environment at any given instant ... is not necessarily one of science fiction. Félix Guattari has imagined a city where one would be able to leave one's apartment, one's street, one's neighborhood, thanks to one's (dividual) electronic card that raises a given barrier; but the card could just as easily be rejected on a given day or between certain hours; what counts is not the barrier but the computer that tracks each person's position—licit or illicit—and effects a universal modulation. (1992: 7)

In other words, bodies within the controlled urban space become data bits in relation to dividual interactions, and the notion of individuality as irreducible unit has become questionable for individuals who are now increasingly 'divided' and reduced to the smallest units by technologies and digital network interfaces. In November 2016, the city of Iruma, Saitama Prefecture in Japan, initiated a project to keep track of the elderly with dementia by tagging them with a scannable barcode sticker.[10] This is a pertinent example of how individuals become data-coded ubiquitous bodies in Japan. Subsuming the unruly dementia body under the surveillance of the city, the dividual gets absorbed into the larger platform of data control under the guise of individual caring. A similar mechanism can be witnessed in the case of the Japanese government's control of Akihabara.

The international spectacle of the city of Tokyo installing CCTV cameras in 2010 after Katō's murderous rampage sent out the message to the world that the unruly otaku,

[10] http://www.bbc.com/news/world-asia-38247437, accessed 15 January 2018.

regardless of whether Katō was an actual otaku or not, was under control. The incident's location in Akihabara itself created a myth of Katō's otaku positionality. Important to remember is that the image of the 'benevolent' otaku in the media that burgeoned since the mid-2000s was partly motivated by the Japanese government's *Cool Japan* policies. Otaku became positive forces as they were deemed as contributing to the wealth of the nation by attracting global, mostly Western, fans to Japan. However, the reality in Japan is that there is what can be described as a 'one-strike-you-are-out' rule that permeates throughout society.[11] Ever since the 1989 Miyazaki incident, the otaku have been under scrutiny and the modicum of positive perception that the otaku had been enjoying until 2010 was immediately threatened by Katō's murder spree. Naturally, a concerted effort by otaku intellectuals to shield and distance the otaku and their sacred space Akihabara from Katō emerged.

Scholars in Japan point to the problematics of the media calling the incident the 'Akihabara Random Massacre' instead of the 'Katō Incident' as encoding bias against and 'scapegoating' of the otaku (Morikawa 2008: 104). Some even assert that Katō chose Akihabara precisely because it is where the 'powerless peaceful sheep – otaku – gather' and that Katō's statement that 'it didn't matter who I killed' was a symptom of Katō's extreme selfishness crushed under diminishing employment opportunities and his deceitful misdirected anger of not being able to kill his own parents, driven by neoliberal pragmatism (Yoshida 2008: 30–31). From these critical accounts, one can see Katō as a non-otaku who victimised the safe space of the otaku and Akihabara rather than an otaku gone wild. In short, by emphasising the location where the murders occurred over Katō as an individual, the media was able to conveniently sensationalise the incident, harking back to the 1989 otaku Miyazaki serial killings. In this process, the most important issue surrounding Katō's rage, the precarious labour conditions of contemporary Japanese youth, was pushed back into obscurity.[12] At the same time, the Katō incident was a stark reminder to the cautious and suspicious Japanese public that the otaku were not to be trusted, and thus must be 'governed'. 'Tagging' Katō as an otaku and the subsequent installation of CCTV surveillance by the city of Tokyo enabled the illusory performance of ubiquitous control over unruly elements, like the 'broken data bits' in *Coil*, in Akihabara.

Interestingly, the Japanese government's desire to create a ubiquitous society and to appeal to global consumers is haunted by many contradictions and the glaring gap from its current digital infrastructure including Internet/cell phone connection and other service industries. Japan may boast the international image of being high-tech, but its bureaucracy continues to pose a serious challenge to the development of a faster and better ubiquitous society. For example, it may still take up to a month to get a new Internet connection in Tokyo (half the time of what it used to take in the mid-2000s) and purchasing a new cell phone is as strenuous as, if not more stringent than, opening a credit card account. At the same time, Japanese smart phones cannot be easily unlocked for international usage. The Internet infrastructure was widely laid out during the early to

[11] This 'one-strike-you-are-out' practice applies to other aspects of Japanese society at large (the massive bullying culture in Japan is also affected by this rule; e.g., if one does not use chopsticks 'correctly' or smile 'correctly', etc. then they are often blacklisted and thus justified to be bullied). This invisible and internalised pressure, I argue, may contribute to the effectiveness of surveillance in Japan.

[12] Slater and Galbraith (2011) examine the online discourse surrounding Katō's murderous rampage and postulate that Katō was depicted as a victim by sympathetic voices. However, the mainstream media in Japan did not cover Katō as a victim.

mid-2000s, and was behind many other developed countries around the world at the time. This national project anticipated the development of the Content industry (shared digital content) as well as ubiquitous society (shared digital network) in the twenty-first century. With this, many forms of governance were discussed by the government, including issues of content copyrights and digital piracy. One other example of governance in relation to the Content industry can be seen in the Tokyo Metropolitan Government's 2010 attempt to 'clean up' the image of manga and anime through passing an ordinance to censor unethical and pornographic images of 'non-existing youths' (*hijitsuzai seishōnen*). Although the Japanese national government excluded manga and anime from the list of media censorship regarding child pornography in 2014, Tokyo holds its own regulation against the freedom of sexual expression in creative narratives. Manga and anime involving incest or vaguely defined 'inappropriate' sexual behaviour is considered harming the youth's moral compass and should be banned. Evoking the Satchi searchmatons in *Coil* that run around the city to erase 'dangerous' data bits that could open doors to the black space that could contaminate the minds of the city dwellers, the city of Tokyo's effort to restrict access to 'dangerous' Content (in whose eyes?) under the ploy to protect the youth population hides the fact that it was the incentive to attract global consumers that motivated the city to this highly contested regulation. Ironically, Tokyo's censorship to desexualise the Content industry contradicts the national government's approach on how to attract global Content consumers.

In 2009, the Ministry of Foreign Affairs, which oversees the global promotion of anime abroad, designated three female 'cute' (*kawaii*) ambassadors, replacing the previous popular culture ambassadors such as the fictional female cat *Hello Kitty* and the futuristic male robot cat *Doraemon*.[13] Although the term for these female ambassadors was only one year, as popular anime images heavily focus on preadolescent-looking girls that appear in high school uniforms or Victorian doll outfits (known as gothic Lolita or *gosurori*), the utilisation of live female bodies to promote the fictional realm of anime by the Japanese government raises serious questions about the governance of female subjectivity in relation to nation branding. According to Laura Miller, the selection of these three females was determined solely by one male bureaucrat (2011: 20). The new female ambassadors, dressed as a high school student, a gothic Lolita, and a Harajuku girl (*gyaru*), visited Japanese embassies around the world and posed in front of avid foreign anime fans. Online sites such as Youtube.com present us with their performances. In London, 2010, the gothic Lolita character Kera appeared on stage and simply twirled around.[14] One scholar who attended one of the cute ambassadors' events reported that a Japanese government official verbally ordered the cute ambassadors to 'twirl round and round!' (*kuru kuru mawatte*!).[15]

Presenting live female bodies as visually appealing 'dolls', as in the aforementioned case of Kera, informs us of the ubiquitous gender governance the Japanese government is practicing in relation to the Content industry. My research on the Content industry during the mid-late 2000s, including numerous interviews with Japanese government officials and

[13]See related news reports: http://www.huffingtonpost.com/2008/05/20/hello-kitty-japans-touris_n_102736.html; http://www.msnbc.msn.com/id/23716592/ns/world_news-asia-pacific/; http://mag.shifteast.com/japan-inducts-ambassadors-of-cute/

[14]http://www.youtube.com/watch?v=lvXbyaW0Rik, accessed 5 October 2017.

[15]This information was presented at a Sophia University workshop in Tokyo, Japan, August 2009.

bureaucrats, reveals that the global fandom of anime imagined by the Japanese policy makers is essentially white males, a possible projection of the imagined homogeneity of Japanese otaku population onto a global scale. In contrast, the image of the Japanese school girl is replete with fetishistic sexual imagination (Miller 2011: 22) and the fashion of the Harajuku girl conjures the image of young sex workers near Shibuya/Harajuku due to the concentration of love hotels and sex workers in the Dōgenzaka area next to Shibuya station. Hence, the designation of 'cute' female ambassadors may have appeared to be an attractive strategy to those bureaucrats who did not realise the limitations, let alone the offensiveness, of sexualising the Content industry into three young female bodies, an approach that Miller aptly defines as the 'pimping of Japan' (Miller 2011). This practice also grossly ignores the heterogeneous global consumers' desires and preferences in relation to the vast array of anime genres. Presenting anime as Japanese *feminine*, embodied in live, sexualised and fantasy-evoking female bodies further confirms the long-lasting Western stereotypes of Japanese women being confined to the realm of 'sex and submission', a century-old image stemming from the narrative of *Madame Butterfly* (Klein 2003: 146).

On the one hand, the government's policy to promote *Cool Japan* to a global audience has united with the vision of a ubiquitous network society where digital content and platforms are integrated to support the Content industry. On the other, this visionary plan has not only reconfigured the urban spaces of Akihabara and Tokyo through the celebratory transformation of otaku male subjectivity, but has also utilised female bodies in anticipation of the imagined global fans' (a.k.a. white males) desires. In other words, Japanese female bodies are to entice global male fans to Japan, and Akihabara as the centre of the creative industries – a virtual register of fantasy and surveillance within Japan – becomes their final destination where they can celebrate their otaku masculinity. As a result, the 'great nation' Japan, as imagined in *Coil*, is ironically built upon the Japanese government's desire to be desired by the white male consumer subjectivity, facilitated by the late neoliberal state of global capitalism.

This point is further evidenced in the explosive increase of Japanese television programmes that feature predominantly Western foreigners either living, visiting or desiring to visit Japan. While programmes such as *Amazing Jipangu!* (*Ame-jipangu!*, 2014 on TBS), *Why did you come to Japan?* (*You wa nani shi ni nihon he*?, 2013, TV Tokyo) were created to offer constant confirmation of Japan's attractiveness to foreigners, titles like *Found in the world village! Japanese in places like this* (*Sekai no mura de hakken! Konna tokoro ni nihonjin*, 2013, Asahi TV) and *Why in the world there? Japanese* (*Sekai naze soko ni? Nihonjin*, 2012, TV Tokyo) were designed to explore remote places around the world where Japanese, predominantly women, have settled, often through marriage, and become active in local communities. In one programme, the entire television crew travels for days to a remote town in India to find the one and only Japanese woman living there. She is married to an Indian man and runs a small hostel, and she has become the 'face' of Japan in that town. Another episode shows a woman in a similar situation, the only difference being that she lives in Africa. Comparable programmes exploring how foreigners view Japan existed in the past, but this purported 'Japan Is Great!' phenomenon, according to Tomomi Yamaguchi, was strengthened visibly after Abe Shinzo's political revival and the nationalist turn in 2012 (2017: 3). Additionally, the International Olympic Committee's 2013 announcement for Tokyo to host the 2020 summer

Olympics game clearly contributed to the increase of these types of programmes. The constant affirmation from 'Western' foreigners that Japan seeks as a nation through these programmes appears to be unquenchable. Interestingly, the majority of the programmes mediate the West through the Japanese female body, mirroring how the Japanese government utilised the cute ambassadors to promote the Content industry. Yet, underneath the message that 'Japan is loved by everybody around the world' exists another layer of 'Japanese are everywhere (even in the deep lands of India and Africa)', which conjures up an illusion of Japan as a truly ubiquitous nation, in a safe and unthreatening manner.

Conclusion

The Japanese government's new promotional policy towards the creative Content industries such as anime, manga and video games in the twenty-first century stemmed mostly from the larger neoliberal capitalist mode of free market flows as part of the process of globalisation during the 1990s. However, as it became combined with the larger governmental plan to actualise a ubiquitous society, the Content industry and the otaku space of Akihabara fell under the larger schema of governance. In order to facilitate a ubiquitous society, the Japanese government has shown little concern for individual subjectivity and privacy. The resulting surveillance of the urban landscape and the pervasive data collection, as seen in the case of Akihabara's CCTVs and the futuristic depiction in the television anime series *Dennō Koiru*, has yet to be challenged by critical discourses both inside and outside of Japan. The Japanese government may imagine a utopian system under the banners of *Cool Japan* and *Ubiquitous Society*. However, living in Japan informs one that Japan is far from actualising this utopian goal. Information and experiences are diverse and fragmented, and navigating through the city can sometimes be as schizophrenic an experience as Fredric Jameson would describe as 'fragmented and schizophrenic decentering and dispersion of [the subject]' (1991: 413).

The broader notion of control in relation to establishing a ubiquitous society has been overshadowed by the celebratory visions of creating a user-friendly environment for the aging population in Japan. However, when the ubiquitous surveillance occurs in spaces such as Akihabara, with the larger awareness/expectation of the global 'male' gaze upon its space, then for whom is the control asserted? As Japan tries to rebuild its past economic glory through the promotion of the Content industry, with the increasing emphasis on traditional culture that appears as rehashing old policies that resulted in self-Orientalisation, the ubiquitous society it envisions may result in total surveillance driven by external sources. This may, far from how the Japanese government imagines, hinder the process of creating 'better lives' for the people who live within the virtual space they have created called 'Japan'.

Acknowledgements

I would like to thank those who provided feedback to earlier versions of this research at the *Performing Space in Asian Film: Interdisciplinary Perspectives* workshop (Singapore, February 2010) and *The Cultural Typhoon Annual Conference* (Tokyo, July 2010). Additionally, I am grateful to Kai-man Chang, Michele White, Justin Wolfe, Edith Wolfe, and Michel Syrimis at Tulane University, Tadashi Anno and Edward Drott at Sophia University, Teri Silvio at Academia Sinica, and the two anonymous reviewers for offering invaluable comments and guidance on this essay.

Disclosure statement

No potential conflict of interest was reported by the author.

Funding

This project received no external funding.

References

Akiba Keizai Shimbun. 2007. *Akibaga Chikyū wo Nomikomu Hi: Akiba Karuchuraru Shinkaron* (The Day Akiba Swallows the Earth: Evolution Theory of Akiba Culture). Tokyo: Kadokawa SS Communications Shinsho.

Azuma, H. 2001. *Dōbutsuka Suru Posutomodan* (Animalizing Postmodern). Tokyo: Kodansha Gendai Shinsho.

Baba, H. 2014. *Ame-jipangu!* (Amazing Jipangu!). Tokyo Broadcasting System Television, Inc. (TBS), Japan.

Caruso, D. J. 2008. *Eagle Eye*. DreamWorks, Goldcrest Pictures, KMP Film Invest, Digital Image Associates, K/O Paper Products, USA, Great Britain, Germany.

Choo, K. 2012. 'Nationalizing 'Cool': Japan's Global Promotion of the Content Industry'. In Nissim Otmazgin and Eyal Ben-Ari (eds), *Popular Culture and the State in East and Southeast Asia*. London: Routledge, 85–105.

Daliot-Bul, M. 2009. 'Japan Brand Strategy: The Taming of 'Cool Japan' and the Challenges of Cultural Planning in the Postmodern Age'. *Social Science Japan Journal* 12:2, 247–66.

Deleuze, G. 1992. 'Postscript on the Societies of Control'. *October* 59, 3–7.

DiMarco, J. 2004. *Computer Graphics and Multimedia: Applications, Problems and Solutions*. Hershey: Idea Group Publishing.

Ernst, T. 2004. 'E-Wheelchair: A Communication System Based on IPv6 and NEMO'. In Daqing Zhang and Mourni Mokhtari (eds), *Toward a Human-Friendly Assistive Environment*. Amsterdam: IOS Press, 213–20.

Galbrath, P. W. 2010. 'Akihabara: Conditioning a Public "Otaku" Image'. *Mechademia* 5:1, 210–30.

geek. 2008. '"Akiba Blog"de Yomu, Kyōkō Zenya no Akihabara de Okotteitakoto' (Reading from 'Akiba Blog': What Happened in Akihabara the Night Before the Violence). In Akiba Tōrima Jiken wo Dō Yomuka? (How to Read the Akiba Random Massacre?). Tokyo: Yosensha Mook.

Haggerty, K. D. and Ericson, R. V. 2006. *The New Politics of Surveillance and Visibility*. Toronto, Buffalo, London: University of Toronto Press.

Hosoda, M. 2009. *Summer Wars*. Madhouse Inc., Japan.

Ibata-Arens, K. C. 2005. *Innovation and Entrepreneurship in Japan: Politics, Organizations, and High Technology Firms*. Cambridge: Cambridge University Press.

Iso, M. 2007. *Dennō Koiru* (Coil A Circle of Children). Bandai Visual Company, Madhouse Inc., NHK Enterprises, Tokuma Shoten, Japan.

Iwabuchi, K. 2002. *Recentering Globalization*. Durham: Duke University Press.

Jameson, F. 1991. *Postmodernism, or, The Cultural Logic of Late Capitalism*. Durham: Duke University Press.

Kato, M. 2013. *You wa Nani Shi ni Nihon he?* (Why Did You Come to Japan?). TV Tokyo Corporation, Japan.

Kellner, D. 2003. *Media Spectacle*. London & New York: Routledge.
Klein, C. 2003. *Cold War Orientalism: Asia in the Middlebrow Imagination 1945–1961*. Berkeley: University of California Press.
Leheny, D. 2006. 'A Narrow Place to Cross Swords: "Soft Power" and the Politics of Japanese Popular Culture in East Asia'. In Peter J Katzenstein and Takashi Shiraishi (eds), *Beyond Japan: The Dynamics of East Asian Regionalism*. Ithaca: Cornell University Press, 211–33.
Liman, D. 2002. *The Bourne Identity*. Universal Pictures, The Kennedy/Marshall Company, Hypnotic, Kalima Productions, GmbH & Co. KG, Stillking Films, USA, Germany, Czech Republic.
Lyon, D. 2004. 'Globalizing Surveillance: Comparative and Sociological Perspectives'. *International Sociology* 19:2, 135–49.
Lyon, D. 2009. *Identifying Citizens: ID Cards as Surveillance*. Cambridge: Polity.
McTeigue, J. 2006. *V for Vendetta*. Warner Bros., Virtual Studios, Silver Pictures, Anarchos Productions, Studio Babelsberg, Medienboard Berlin-Brandenburg, DC Comics, USA, Great Britain, Germany.
Miller, L. 2011. 'Cute Masquerade and the Pimping of Japan'. *International Journal of Japanese Sociology* 20:1, 18–29.
Ministry of Economy, Trade and Industry. 2004. Strategies for Creating New Industries Report, May.
Ministry of Internal Affairs and Communications. 2006. u-Japan Development Plan Report. June.
Mirzoeff, N. 2006. 'Network Subjects: or, The Ghost is the Message'. In Wendy Hui Kyong Chun and Thomas Keenan (eds), *New Media, Old Media: A History and Theory Reader*. London: Routledge, 335–46.
Miyazaki, H. 1988. *My Neighbor Totoro*. Studio Ghibli, Japan.
Miyazaki, H. 2001. *Spirited Away*. Studio Ghibli, Japan.
Morikawa, K. 2003. *Toshi no Tanjō: Moeru Toshi Akihabara* (Learning from Akihabara: The Birth of a Personapolis). Tokyo: Gentosha.
Morikawa, K. 2008. 'Naze Akiba ga Hankō no Butai ni Erabaretanoka'. In *Akiba Tōrima Jiken wo Dō Yomuka?* (How to Read the Akiba Random Massacre?). Tokyo: Yosensha Mook, 104–06.
Murakami, S. 2005. *Densha Otoko* (Train Man). Toho Company, Fuji Television Network, Hakuhodo DY Media Partners, Kyodo Television, Stardust Picture, Japan.
Murakami, T. 2007. 'Ubiquitous Society in Japan'. In Toshio Obi (ed), *E-Governance: A Global Perspective on a New Paradigm*. Amsterdam: IOS Press, 10–5.
Niccol, A. 1997. *Gattaca*. Columbia Pictures Corporation, Jersey Films, USA.
Nishio, T. 2013. *Sekai no Mura de Hakken! Konna Tokoro ni Nihonjin* (Found in the World Village! Japanese in Places Like This). Asahi Broadcasting Corporation, Japan.
Roquet, P. 2016. 'From Animation to Augmentation: *Dennō Coil* and the Composited Self'. *Animation: An Interdisciplinary Journal* 11:3, 228–45.
Sato, J. 1992. *Sailor Moon*. TV Asahi, Toei Advertising LTD., Toei Animation, Japan.
Sconce, J. 2000. *Haunted Media: Electronic Presence From Telegraphy to Television*. Durham: Duke University Press.
Scott, T. 1998. *Enemy of the State*. Touchstone Pictures, Jerry Bruckheimer Films, Don Simpson/Jerry Bruckheimer Films, Scott Free Productions, USA.
Senoh, K. 2007. *Akiba wo Purodyu-su: Saikaihatsu Purojekuto Gonenkan no Kiseki* (Producing Akiba: The Miracle of 5 Years of Redevelopment). Tokyo: ASCII Shinsho.
Slater, D. and Galbraith, P. W. 2011. 'Re-Narrating Social Class and Masculinity in Neoliberal Japan: An Examination of the Media Coverage of the 'Akihabara Incident' of 2008'. *Electronic Journal of Contemporary Japanese Studies*. Available online at www.japanesestudies.org.uk/articles/2011/SlaterGalbraith.html (accessed 2 November 2017).
Spielberg, S. 2002. *Minority Report*. Twentieth Century Fox, DreamWorks, Cruise/Wagner Productions, Blue Tulip Productions, Ronald Shusett/Gary Goldman, Digital Image Associates, USA.
Stefik, M. and Stefik, B. 2004. *Breakthrough: Stories and Strategies of Radical Innovation*. Cambridge: MIT Press.

Steinberg, M. 2009. 'Anytime, Anywhere Tetsuwan Atomu Stickers and the Emergence of Character Merchandizing'. *Theory, Culture & Society* 26:2–3, 113–38.

Takano, M. 2012. *Sekai Naze Soko ni? Nihonjin* (Why in the World There? Japanese). TV Tokyo Corporation, Japan.

Wan, J. 2015. *Furious 7*. Universal Pictures, Media Rights Capital (MRC), China Film Co., Original Film, One Race Rilms, Dentsu, Fuji Television Network, Québec Production Services Tax Credit, Colorado Office of Film, Television & Media, Abu Dhabi Film Commission, USA, China, Japan, Canada, United Arab Emirates.

Wimmer, K. 2002. *Equilibrium*. Dimension Films, Blue Tulip Productions, USA.

Yamaguchi, T. 2017. 'The "Japan Is Great!" Boom, Historical Revisionism, and the Government'. *The Asia-Pacific Journal: Japan Focus* 12:6–3, 1–6.

Yoshida, T. 2008. 'Shinjiyūshugi Jidai wo Shōchō suru Jikochū Satsujin'. In *Akiba Tōrima Jiken wo Dō Yomuka?* (How to Read the Akiba Random Massacre?). Tokyo: Yosensha Mook, 29–39.

Yuyama, K. 1997. *Pokémon*. TV Tokyo, SOFTX, Shogakukan-Shueisha Productions Co., Ltd., Japan.

4 Nation branding in contemporary Taiwan: a grassroots perspective

Adina Simona Zemanek

ABSTRACT
This paper, based on textual analysis and interviews, offers a complementary perspective of scholarly studies of nation branding which focus on the state and corporate elites involved in such undertakings. It places grassroots initiatives in branding Taiwan through tourist souvenirs and other video and graphic materials against the larger background of cultural policies and official branding campaigns, and shows grassroots actors' complex entanglement with official institutions, policies and discourses despite declared scepticism towards the latter and a low degree of direct collaboration. It compares official and grassroots messages and argues that the latter are more coherent; capture a local specificity and encourage a tourist gaze centred around the 'human touch' theme; distance themselves from China, the significant 'other' of Taiwanese nationalism; and markedly highlight an epistemological and representational strategy based on individual, sensorial experience, which may constitute a response to biased and untrustworthy state national narratives of the martial law era.

1. Introduction

The nation is an ever-changing narration constituted by stories that intersect or compete with each other (Berger, Eriksonas and Mycock 2008). This concept's inherent indeterminacy has been especially visible in Taiwan during the last decades. Mark Harrison speaks of Taiwanese identity as an incessant imperative and open-ended discursive process (2009: 58) expressed in a multitude of politically constitutive, partial and negotiated narratives. Hegemonic stories are formulated by academics who inscribe Taiwan within dominant epistemes (China or Western modernity), and taken over by polarised party politics that reproduces these structures of domination (Harrison 2015). The ideology-laden official public diplomacy reflects these divergent standpoints. Shifts in strategic agendas with each succession of ruling parties, combined with a lack of central coordination and consensus between various government departments, have constituted the main impediments to formulating a consistent brand image for Taiwan (Rawnsley 2014). However, the stories put forward by formal knowledge makers coexist with other meaningful, albeit marginal narratives that contest dominant structures, engage with memory and reflect people's lived, everyday experiences of Taiwan's transformation and modernisation (Harrison 2015).

Such stories situated outside the state and authoritative political, intellectual or scholarly discourses constitute the main concern of this paper. While Berger, Eriksonas and Mycock's book investigates competing historical narratives from the viewpoint of national representation, my argument adopts a different theoretical framework – that of nation branding – which offers a set of concepts relevant for my case studies and a comparative perspective useful for delineating Taiwanese particularities. The exact meaning of nation branding has been hotly disputed, to the extent that it can be deemed 'an ideological construction of its practitioners and scholars'. However, its definitions consistently mention 'discourses and practices located at the intersection of economy, culture and politics' (Kaneva 2012: 4–5). Their aim is 'the creation and communication of national identity using tools, techniques, and expertise from the world of corporate brand management' (Aronczyk 2013: 16), in order to highlight a nation's unique character and increase its global competitiveness (Aronczyk 2009: 292). Critical scholars of nation branding (a trend with which this paper aligns itself) borrow Bourdieu's field theory and examine actors motivated by various interests, striving for desired positions and assets (Kaneva 2012: 15). Similarly, the actors central to my study formulate consistent definitions of Taiwaneseness that interpellate local and international consumers. As active brand managers, they skilfully exploit new resources created by state cultural policies in order to broaden the circulation of their messages and ensure identification with them among the addressees.

Many researchers explore a region where nation branding has rapidly proliferated: Central and East European countries, faced with the need to (re)formulate themselves and gain global visibility as nations after the collapse of communist regimes, while also undergoing economic and political transition and coming to terms with a traumatic past. These factors caused 'a state of inadequacy' affecting both individual psychologies and political decisions (Kaneva 2012: 6–7). Under such circumstances, the crisis of national representation involved a transition of yet another kind, 'between a shameful and a desired identity' (Kaneva 2012: 7). The latter is interlinked with a long-standing ideological dichotomy between East and West. The revaluation of the West as a model to be emulated underlies these countries' readiness to import the 'gospel of nation branding' and to commission such projects to UK and US consultants (Kaneva 2012: 7–8). Given Taiwan's recent history, international status, quest for a local identity, and nation branding initiatives, the ideas above constitute a valuable frame of reference. Nevertheless, my study will not highlight resemblances but areas less exposed in existing research and elements that can be considered specific to Taiwan.

Nation branding scholars focus on the field of power and three categories of actors: state institutions commissioning branding projects to a 'transnational promotional class' (Aronczyk 2013: 39), and local dominant elites (technocrats and marketing professionals) conniving with the state in order to share in the profits (Surowiec 2012: 127). Their concerted efforts are aimed at constructing and promoting positive, coherent images abroad and ensuring allegiance for them at home. Unlike older countries, with national images well-established among audiences both at home and abroad, new nations struggle with significant challenges: alternative narratives circulated by global media (Saunders 2012; Bardan and Imre 2012), deeply-rooted earlier discourses (Graan 2016: 88), or strong domestic opposition (Graan 2016; Bardan and Imre 2012). Much nation branding research emphasises elite hegemony and the exclusion of specific local groups or the general public from democratic participation in branding projects (Aronczyk 2009, 2013; Pamment 2015; Graan 2016). Official versions of national identity reproduce and commodify stereotypes for an external 'tourist gaze' while marginalising the lived experiences of actual national communities. Domestic campaigns position their addressees as 'cultural ambassadors' embodying brand-related values, thus seeking to regulate performances of national identity.

Paradoxically, critical studies tend to overlook grassroots agents as sources of branding messages. They mostly elaborate on elites associated with the field of state power and their practices of designing and implementing branding images or strategies. Accounts of disruptive narratives concern Western sources (Saunders 2012; Bardan and Imre 2012); studies of domestic publics focus on state regulation of brand performance (Graan 2016); voices of dissent are seen as antagonistic reactions triggered by state initiatives (Graan 2016; Bardan and Imre 2012). Similarly, works on cultural policies and nation branding in Taiwan favour state institutions and initiatives (Chang 2006) or top-level politicians (Hughes 2014, who refers to Taiwan's former president Ma Ying-jeou and Lung Ying-tai, former minister of culture). Publications on nation branding in Taiwan analyse texts produced by government agencies (Liao 2014), assess existing branding efforts and present survey-based theme proposals for tourism campaigns (Chen 2014; Zhang and Wang 2000). My article adopts a complementary perspective: it turns towards grassroots tourist souvenir designers as alternative narrators who contribute to constructing the brand 'Taiwan' in the sense of 'a cluster of strategic cultural ideas', of 'functional and emotional values' that guarantee a positive and unique experience and differentiate it from other entities (Dinnie 2008: 14). It will assess the extent of these actors' unruliness towards the branding regime and show that their relationship with the state cannot be reduced to simple antagonism.

My discussion of state and grassroots branding messages will refer to John Urry and Jonas Larsen's concept of the tourist gaze – a cultural practice that 'orders, shapes and classifies, rather than reflects the world', a socially acquired and conditioned way of seeing based on contrast with home spaces and everyday work (2011: 2–3). It implies the collection of signs representing a national character or local identity (2011: 15–16), and is determined by the media and tourism industries that construct 'visitor attractions'. The range of places with this status changes over time: the postmodern fusion of high and low culture has given rise to interest in vernacular architecture and work-related spaces or artefacts (2011: 98, 124, 139–141). I will argue that Taiwanese souvenir designers consistently employ mundane, vernacular sights and objects that usually go unnoticed, and de-naturalise them in order to define Taiwaneseness as object of the tourist gaze. Such elements of everyday life shape national identity as understood by Edensor (2002): a particular lifestyle and sense of belonging linked to a familiar environment. Edensor emphasises the performative character of national identity, which is enacted through culturally determined, unreflexive, shared codes and procedures, related to habitual actions performed in private and public spaces: styles of clothing, demeanour, daily routines (washing, eating, working, driving etc.). Urry and Larsen also highlight the bodily, multi-sensuous, affective and performative aspect of the tourist experience (2011: 189–190). Performativity and bodily involvement are salient elements of the strategies used for constructing a particular type of tourist gaze in the grassroots texts I analyse.

2. Cultural policies and nation branding in Taiwan

In post-World War II Taiwan, culture has constituted a key building block for national identity, and a significant stake in struggles for political power and legitimacy. Changes in dominant factions and ruling parties gave rise to new cultural policies, formulated as reactions against previous hegemonic frameworks. From the mid-1940s, the KMT government promoted Chinese culture in order to legitimise its claim to mainland China and counteract the effects of Japan's colonial assimilation policy. The 1960s' Cultural Renaissance Movement (a response to the Cultural Revolution) constructed Taiwan as the last bastion of traditional Chinese culture under destruction in the PRC. In the 1980s, Chiang Ching-kuo's political reforms inaugurated de-Sinicisation in favour of the hitherto marginalised indigenous culture. The Taiwanisation process intensified after the lifting of martial law (1987). During the 1990s, KMT chairman and ROC president Lee Teng-hui officially promoted local culture, thus replacing China with Taiwan as a homeland and symbolic centre of national identification (Chang 2006). Chen Shui-bian, the DPP president who came into power in 2000, continued his predecessor's policy of loyalty to Taiwan. Ma Ying-jeou's presidency (2008–2016) inaugurated a more conciliatory stance towards the PRC, manifested in strengthened cross-strait business ties and a return to the idea of Taiwan as preserver of classical Chinese culture. Ma's inclusion of the Taiwanese into a 'Chinese nation' (中華民族), his advocacy of Confucian ethics and the increased proportion of Classical Chinese (文言) and Chinese history in the high school curriculum triggered protests against 'de-Taiwanisation' (Hsiau 2012: 108, Hughes 2014: 123–124). By contrast, current president Tsai Ing-wen's culture-related programme emphatically reinstates the DPP's Taiwan-centered cultural policy (2015).

State endorsement for the local arts and cultural industries began in the 1990s. Upon its advent to power, the DPP distanced itself from KMT-supported high culture and time-honoured folklore. Instead, it promoted the cultural and creative industries and emphasised their economic potential (Lu 2002: 43–47; Chang 2006: 193). It was also during this period that tourism became an official priority (Chang 2006: 193–195) and the first nation branding projects were initiated. In 2002, the Ministry of Economic Affairs, the Ministry of Education, the Council for Cultural Affairs and the Government Information Office were entrusted with developing the creative industries and constructing a modern, unique image of Taiwan for international promotion through branding and marketing techniques (2006: 195–197). Simultaneously, the Tourism Bureau launched a campaign with the slogan 'Taiwan, Touch Your Heart' accompanied by a logo featuring the island's map and the word 'Taiwan' in coloured letters whose shapes carried symbolic meanings. Despite official public diplomacy initiatives that downplayed Taiwan's local specificity, Ma Ying-jeou's presidency unvaryingly emphasised tourism, albeit with a shift towards PRC tourists and students. In 2011 the 'Taiwan, Touch Your Heart' campaign was revamped as 'Taiwan – The Heart of Asia', with a new logo designed by the London-based company Winkreative.

Given Taiwan's democratic culture, the state is not the only actor that engages in public diplomacy. It cannot effectively control non-state discourses, nor ensure uniformity among its own narratives, coming from sources with different agendas. Cultural policies may prove unable to influence ongoing trends in public opinion, such as the rise in declared Taiwanese (as opposed to Chinese) identity (Hughes 2014: 131). They may also elicit unintended behaviour, such as positive interpretations of the KMT past enabled by the 'de-Chiang-Kai-shek-ification' movement since the 1990s (Taylor 2010: 189–190). Academic studies reveal dissatisfaction with government actions, suspicion or distrust towards state agencies, or prevalent scepticism with the KMT and DPP's ideologies, perceived as 'indistinguishable' by social and political activists (Ho 2014: 101; Hughes 2014: 130–131). Non-state actors enjoy more credibility and engage in public diplomacy outside the shifting dominant ideologies (Rawnsley 2014: 168–170). Chen Shui-bian's first inaugural speech assigned a key role to grassroots organisations in the construction of Taiwanese culture (Hughes 2014: 121). Tsai Ing-wen's programme also emphasises the need for democratic participation in cultural governance (2015). The branding actors discussed in this paper are wary of party politics, position themselves outside the state and participate in activities usually associated with the civil society. However, they cannot be included in the latter sphere. Instead, they can be seen as acting within an intermediary space – that of *minjian* (民間), explored by Chen (2010: 224–245).

3. Research method

Critical studies of nation branding investigate actors' interests, their struggle for desired positions and resources, their self-defined roles and actions, and the texts (slogans, logos or other visual elements) resulting from branding practices. My study shows grassroots actors' motivations for branding Taiwan, their connections to state policies, institutions and initiatives, their perception of Taiwan's specificity and the strategies they employ in conveying it to the audience through a specific form of 'tourist gaze'. It is informed by discourse analysis, which studies the social production of knowledge and its evolution within a broader economic, political and social context, as well as the dynamics of power and ideology involved in meaning-making processes (Phillips and Hardy 2002). Critical discourse analysis combines the study of discourses and texts with fieldwork and ethnography (Wodak 2001: 69); my empirical data consists of collected texts and interviews with their authors.

Tourism is one of the key spheres that nation branding involves, and the two major Taiwanese branding campaigns were initiated by the ROC Tourism Bureau. This study will also focus on tourism-related texts: souvenirs (postcards, refrigerator magnets, bookmarks, glass coasters etc.) collected between February and October 2014 in Taipei and New Taipei City. A significant share of the market was held by 'classical' souvenirs depicting motifs that Edensor (2002: 40) terms a 'national landscape ideology', i.e., natural or man-made iconic sites already imbued with national significance, cityscapes representing (national) modernity, or aboriginal folk culture. Many other objects featured everyday home or city sights. The latter category included nostalgia-tinted images from the Japanese colonial period, the 1960s and 1970s, and contemporary Taiwan. I chose to focus on souvenirs depicting present-day mundane sights, a sizeable and increasing market niche: follow-up fieldwork in 2016 and 2017 revealed numerous new producers. Despite the diversity of sources, such souvenirs convey a coherent message, reflected in their designers' other creative works and in texts by other authors (picture books, graphic novels etc.).

Between March and May 2017, I conducted in-depth, semi-structured interviews (in Chinese) with three souvenir designers and company owners, aimed at assessing their stances towards official cultural policies and nation branding projects, potential collaboration with state institutions, creative principles, sales channels and customers. I complemented the interviews with materials available on these companies' websites and in other media. The three companies (6636 Advertising & Creativity, Miin Design Co. Ltd. and eyeDesign[1]) were established in 2005–2007 and are small-scale with two to ten employees, one designer (6636 and eyeDesign) or a designer team (Miin). Taiwan-themed souvenirs are central to Miin Design's activity; eyeDesign combines them with other Taiwan-related tasks, and they only constitute a sideline for 6636 Advertising & Creativity. All three companies also take up commissioned projects. Miin Design offers a large range of products (postcards, greeting cards, refrigerator magnets, bookmarks etc.) grouped into thematic and stylistic series and distributed throughout Taiwan through the Eslite network, souvenir shops at tourist locations and airports, small bookstores, and hotel stores. After several years of unsuccessful attempts to market his souvenirs (glass coasters, cups, shopping bags, backpacks, and others) at Taipei department stores, tourist sites and museum shops, Ariel (6636s owner) started a lasting collaboration with duty-free shops at Taoyuan and Songshan airports, and recently with Taipei 101. EyeDesign's Frog sells his postcards and wooden souvenirs at his store in a Taipei tourist area.

Despite their generational closeness (Ariel was born in the 1960s, Ben and Frog – in the early 1970s), my interviewees differ in appearance and personality. Ariel's casual dressing style and Mandarin interspersed with English embody Taiwan's cultural hybridity. Ben is always on the watch for international trends, searching for new forms of expression. Frog is a strong individualist and travel aficionado. Their works reach a diverse, foreign and local audience. Frog targets Taiwanese white-collar fans of mountain hiking and cycling, and Hong Kong tourists. Westerners and Japanese are the main target audience of Ben, Miin Design's owner, but his customers include Taiwanese people. Initially, Ariel did not consider specific addressees, but his souvenirs are now successful with Asian tourists (Thailand, Malaysia, Hong Kong). Significantly, none of them targets PRC tourists, who until recently visited Taiwan in package tours and were interested in other topics (Chiang Kai-shek's legacy and anti-communist propaganda). With three in-depth case studies, this paper offers a glance at the intricacies of grassroots nation branding in present-day Taiwan. Rather than confirming existing patterns, the overlapping areas between the chosen samples can open new paths for more extensive research.

4. Motivation for branding Taiwan

All interviewed designers displayed strong personal engagement in promoting Taiwan and a sense of mission. Ben and Frog described experiences of travel shaping a salient Taiwanese identity that became a key incentive for their branding work. Three weeks spent in Barcelona in 2004 made Ben aware of resemblances between Catalonia and Taiwan – their ambiguous political status, pursuit of independence, and a tendency for external observers to overlook their local identities while incorporating them into culturally related, larger entities internationally recognised as states: Spain and China. Frog obtained knowledge on Taiwan's geography (marginalised during the martial law era) through an individual, empowering, first-hand method which he perceives to have been previously

[1]The company names and owners' pseudonyms are used with their permission.

disparaged by both state and family education. His round-the-island cycling trips (the first at 17, in 1989, and others in his 30s) ultimately inspired him to renounce his managerial job at a large IT company and focus on Taiwan-centred design. Ariel did not conceive his mission at a national level but on a smaller scale, as recording and disseminating collective memories of a vernacular city architecture menaced with gradual demise by ongoing modernisation.

The three designers insist on branding Taiwan on their own terms, with little regard for popularity and material success. Ariel's souvenir series was initially non-profitable and is still secondary to his advertising business. Nevertheless, he persistently uses himself as a model for his bags or other accessories, and incessantly seeks new sales channels. Moreover, he often 'smuggles' similar representational strategies into other forms of creative work. Ben's innovative approach to design and marketing strategies have made his souvenirs highly successful and central to his business. But rather than simply responding to market demands, he leads trends by consistently promoting a specific kind of tourist gaze and certain favourite themes, not all of which are bestsellers. Frog only accepts commissioned design projects that place Taiwan under the spotlight. The factors that make possible their uncompromising attitude and perseverance in what appears to be a risky endeavour will be provided later.

5. Relationship to state cultural policy and branding campaigns

Despite declared antagonism towards party politics, the state and political elites, my interviewees do express political stances, but emphatically restrict their scope to creative work and private life. Ariel protested against the Taipei Arena in 2015 and mayor Ko Wen-je's plans to do away with illegal extensions and low-rise apartment blocks. He did so personally and through a series of themed drawings posted online and shared with a tree protection foundation for concerted actions. Ben joined public protests against nuclear power, and privately advocates Taiwan's independence. Frog's company website and Facebook profile include slogans against nuclear power and supporting Taiwanese independence. He participated in the 2014 Sunflower Movement, which further strengthened his Taiwanese identity.

Their Taiwan-promoting activities are conducted without official sanction or involvement, and they explicitly assume a position outside or critical towards the state. However, their actual relation to state cultural policies and official branding discourses is one of entanglement, a term borrowed from Marita Sturken's reflections on cultural memory and the historical state apparatus (1997: 5). State policies favouring the cultural and creative industries have benefited these designers' work, although they criticised certain aspects related to actual policy implementation. While none of them actively seeks cooperation with the state, Ariel and Ben have made several small-scale contributions to official projects.

A large company entrusted with producing a promotional video for the 'Taiwan: Touch Your Heart' campaign commissioned Ariel to create the story board. The video was released in 2007 and featured boy band F4, whose members had starred in the 2003 TV drama *Meteor Garden*, successful throughout East and Southeast Asia. Ariel negatively assessed this collaboration: the combination of music stars and tourist sites was forced and the video was behind the times, as F4 had already split and each singer was shot separately. The video failed to capture Taiwan's specificity. Instead of presenting a unique, original perspective, it assembled sights that may have been taken from 'an image bank':

> [Y]ou've got to show them what's the really unique point ... [instead of] some boring visuals. If they can Google that, it means you do nothing. Like this, it's just too convenient; you have to bring up something that people cannot Google.

He also deplored the low remuneration for his contribution and constraints imposed on his creative freedom: the producer decided what tourist sites should be covered, and significantly altered his original story.

The Tourism Bureau under the Ministry of Transportation and Communications and the Taipei City Government's Department of Information and Tourism, already acquainted with Ben's work, approached him for designing a cycling scarf and a series of souvenir and stationery products. These projects did not generate much income for Ben's company (both were below the amount required for public bidding), but allowed him to bring in favourite topics and visual strategies. Ben deplored the difficulties currently encountered by individual designers and small companies competing for state funding, the lack of expertise displayed by civil servants who appoint evaluation committees, and lack of elasticity as to the awardees' use of funds. However, he praised the state's general orientation towards the cultural and creative industries for raising the status of graphic design and for creating a context that spurred the development of applied arts in Taiwan. He also positively evaluated the 'Heart of Asia' logos for the visual novelty they introduced: drawings instead of photographs, in a style he found affinity with. But although the campaign mobilised a diverse and comprehensive array of images to represent Taiwan, he found them superficial and repetitive.

Frog was strongly reluctant to seek involvement in state-led nation branding due to what he perceived as procedural problems: an emphasis on conformity with formal criteria, established values and images; reinforcement of these stereotypical representations by design companies bidding for state projects which strive to fulfil state expectations at the expense of originality; and a hierarchy-based evaluation process informed by non-specialist opinions. Nevertheless, he was familiar with official videos promoting Taiwan and employed them as a term of reference for alternative, similarly themed video advertisements.

6. Branding activity expanding beyond tourist products

These designers' activity is not limited to tourist souvenirs. It is interlinked with other fields, thus forming networks which ensure the presence of similar themes and representational techniques in products not related to the tourism industry, the promotion of these artists and their branding projects in Taiwan, and entanglement with official discourses in ways other than discussed above.

The interviewed designers seem to be well-known media figures. A large amount of information on their companies, creative work (tourist souvenirs and other kinds of products), target audience and marketing strategies, activities in other fields (public lectures, published books, charitable or volunteer work, social activism etc.), lifestyle and worldview has been circulated since around 2009 through many local media outlets catering for a Taiwanese audience and foreigners living in Taiwan, as well as for interested global audiences. These outlets include small-scale personal blogs and independent student media websites,

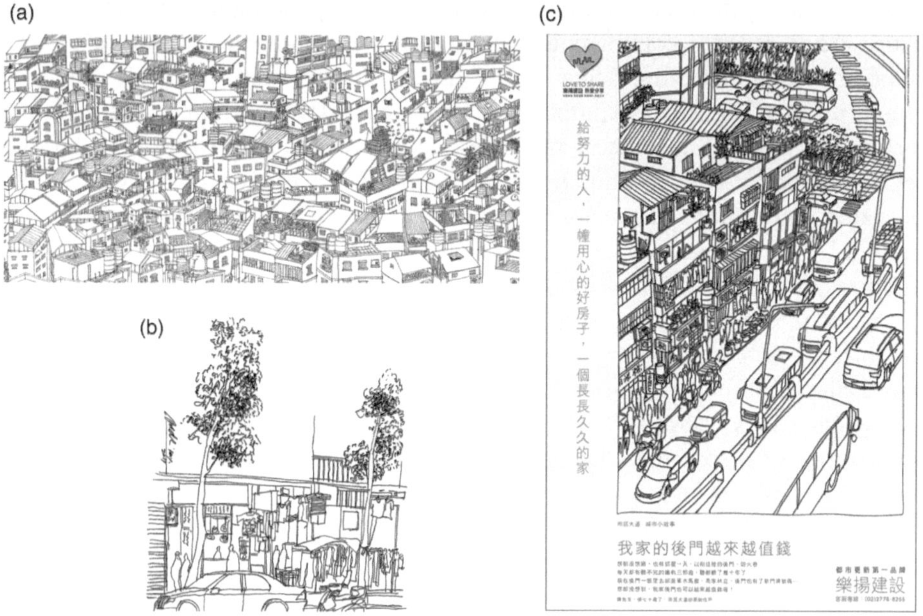

Figure 1. Similar images as different products: image serving as basis for Ariel's 'Rooftops' tourist souvenir series (a), his drawing for a community-building event (b), and his urban renewal newspaper advertisement (c). © 2017 6636 Advertising&Creativity.

portals dedicated to Taiwan and the creative industries, websites of companies that commissioned these designers' projects (in Chinese), as well as major daily newspapers: the Chinese-language *China Times* (中國時報) and *Apple Daily* (蘋果日報), and the English-language *Taipei Times*. These artists' media personas are built around their commitment to promoting Taiwan, which reinforces their position as nation branding agents. Some media channels are targeted at a niche audience or are maintained by actors with interests similar to my interviewees', but many of them are addressed to the general public. Hence it can be inferred that these designers' conspicuous media presence may be due to the widespread popularity of initiatives related to defining national identity, in an official context that encourages both this undertaking and a plurality of voices joining in the identity discourse.

Despite moderate success with marketing his souvenirs, Ariel has found alternative dissemination channels for his black and white drawings of urban sights to highly receptive targets, thus making them visible in actual, virtual and media-related public spaces (Figure 1). He designed a series of products illustrated with trees in an old-style courtyard (large-format wallpapers, table mats, napkins and notebooks) which he donated to his mother's elderly care centre. Thus, without incurring any expense, the centre could bring familiar neighbourhood scenes to people unable to access such places on their own. Ariel also employed everyday urban sights for a project commissioned by a medical clinic. Its owner is a fan of Ariel's drawing style and entrusted him with designing the interior of each newly opened branch. His chaotically clustered, dilapidated, four-storey apartment blocks and views of narrow streets were published in 2011 and 2012 as a series of full-page newspaper ads, accompanied by stories of elderly people complaining about their current living conditions and expressing their wish for modern facilities. The ads were commissioned by construction companies involved in urban renewal projects, aimed at replacing old buildings with new, safer ones while compensating home owners. The unconventional hand drawing form with its human, personal touch was appreciated by the advertisers and struck an emotional chord with their addressees. Ariel also participated in community-building projects.[2] He designed a series of highly appreciated giveaway products for an event promoting his Taipei neighbourhood organised by a well-known bank and sponsored by the city government's Department of Cultural Affairs. In 2011, he was contacted by the same institution (already familiar with his style) to take part in an event concerning the same neighbourhood, for which he authored a notebook illustrated with local sights, gave volunteer guided tours and lectures. Significantly, the foundation which co-organised that event displays one of his drawings on its website.

Frog's creative work reflects his hobbies of mountain climbing and around-the-island cycling trips, both strongly promoted by the state. He first circulated travel narratives and photographs in a book designed as a cycling diary, on Facebook and a personal webpage. Their popularity made Frog aware of a potentially large Taiwanese public interested in learning more about their country. Taking advantage of official support for such initiatives categorised as 'culture and creativity' (文創), he established two coffee shops intended as community-building spaces for travel-related photograph exhibitions and discussions. Later, he closed them down to focus on tourist souvenirs – postcards with photographs from his trips and wood products bearing adventure-inspiring slogans or conceived as educational games based on Taiwan's geography. He is also invited by corporations, schools or other institutions to give talks regarding his hobbies and career. He takes on commissioned projects, but carefully selects them according to his principles of creative freedom and commitment to defining Taiwan. Such cooperation has resulted in video advertisements that convey Taiwan's specificity, shot during travels on various locations. They were commissioned by a Taiwanese recording company, an apparel brand, and an international producer of electric home appliances wishing to localise its image. They mainly portray people whose unconventional life and career choices have recently become popular, and fall under the category of creativity understood as new, sustainable business models aimed at revitalising Taiwan's countryside[3]: young, well-educated urbanites who renounce high-income jobs for organic farming or volunteer work with aboriginal tribes. In an article published by a lifestyle magazine in 2016, Frog presents his own creative work as advertising that of such people. All of them contribute to a new model of tourism catering to customers interested in work- and culinary-based, first-hand travel experiences in small localities. Its marketing strategy is based on new media, which ensure fast information exchange within networks of similar entrepreneurs.

Finally, Ben's works enhance the visibility and profitability of Taiwanese traditional culture. He purchased reproduction rights for Li Tian-lu's famous glove puppetry scene,

[2]The 'community construction' movement (社區總體營造) was initiated in 1995 and is still thriving. It aims at encouraging people's involvement in building local communities closely knit with their architectural and natural environment (Chang 2006: 189–190).

[3]The link between farming, tourism and state promotion of the cultural and creative industries is explored at length by You (2013).

placed on one of his postcards. He also approached the Rixing Type Foundry, renowned for its most extant collection of traditional Chinese movable characters in the world, and commissioned lead types attached to another postcard series.

7. Coherence of official and grassroots branding messages

This section compares the interviewed designers' works with texts from the 'Heart of Asia' campaign: a series of heart-shaped logos, other graphic and video promotional materials available on the Tourism Bureau website4, 'Bravo!' and 'Welcome to Taiwan!' posters displayed on airports.

The visual materials available on the Tourism Bureau website feature many tourist sites listed in official surveys of popularity[5]. The 'Heart of Asia' logos contain many Chinese elements, which may reflect the official cultural policy during Ma Ying-jeou's presidency, when the campaign was launched: buildings resembling the Chiang Kai-shek and Sun Yat-sen Memorial Halls, an imperial guardian lion, the Taipei 101 whose design includes many Chinese auspicious symbols, red lanterns, and tea. Tea is also highlighted on a 'Bravo!' poster, which incorporates Taiwan's history into that of China's opium wars by mentioning the 'Oriental Beauty variety said to be named after Queen Victoria'. Recurrent local foods and agricultural products (rice, pineapple, tea, bananas, watermelons, oranges etc.) reinforce Taiwan's stereotype as snack heaven. The heart logos also feature Taiwan's high-tech electronic products. The cultural and creative industries are represented by dancers in black clothes alluding to the Cloud Gate Dance Company, and Zhu Ming's taichi sculpture series. Picturesque nature constitutes yet another prominent topic. It is sometimes accompanied by aboriginal culture and often serves as background for cycling. Many videos promote the local bicycle brand Giant and official efforts at developing social awareness and infrastructure related to this sport. Although people are referred to as Taiwan's best tourist asset (in what has become a set expression), this theme is insufficiently developed: images of ordinary people are mostly absent.

The 'Heart of Asia' campaign reflects officially endorsed topics and an outsider's gaze upon Taiwan. Instead of building a unique identification, it reinforces activities and sites already popular with foreign tourists and displays the 'generic, clichéd quality of much nation branding messaging' (Graan 2016: 84) through commonly exploited themes: natural beauty, folk traditions, modernity or food. It does not propose an alternative for the Chinese identity upheld during the martial law era, but assimilates such national representations notwithstanding their perception among the Taiwanese public. In a study on ideas of stateness, state territory and national identity produced as a result of group tourism from mainland China to Taiwan, Ian Rowen (2014) shows that PRC tourists identified with local people as fellow Chinese nationals. They incorporated Taiwanese sites into China, as the tour packages they purchased reproduced patterns of travelling in the PRC. 'Scenic spots' (Sun Moon Lake, Alishan) feature water and mountains, a

[4]Taiwan.net.tw (acessed 27 June 2017).

[5]The '2015 Annual Survey Report on Visitors' Expenditure and Trends in Taiwan' (available online: http://admin.taiwan.net.tw/upload/statistic_eng/20160810/746f0cac-3cfe-494e-8dd5-ccf8e34477ce.pdf; accessed 27 June 2017) lists the following ranking of sites popular with foreign tourists: (1) night markets; (2) Taipei 101; (3) the National Palace Museum; (4) the Chiang Kai-shek Memorial Hall; (5) the Sun Moon Lake; (6) Kending National Park; (7) Jiufen; (8) Dr. Sun Yat-sen Memorial Hall; (9) Tianxiang Recreation Area of Taroko National Park; (10) Taipei's Ximending (p. ix).

To see logos for the 'Taiwan – The Heart of Asia' campaign by the Tourism Bureau, Ministry of Transportation and Communications, Republic of China, please visit https://eng.taiwan.net.tw/m1.aspx?sNo=0000219 and follow the link to Heart-Shaped Cards. Some images are reproduced in the original journal article.

combination legitimised by a long tradition of landscape painting. A similar role was played by shows of aboriginal cultures, or sites commemorating figures and events significant both for PRC and Taiwan's history. By contrast, local people confronted with the presence of large PRC tour groups felt alienated from the above-mentioned areas and de-territorialised them as Taiwanese by deliberately avoiding them.

On the contrary, the interviewed grassroots actors re-territorialise Taiwan, so that the images they construct are locally relevant as well. According to Ben, Taiwan's cultural diversity makes it difficult to pinpoint a local specificity. Ariel spoke of Taiwan's hybrid, cosmopolitan culture and the impossibility of finding a local flavour either in its history (traditions) or in its modern art and fashion. As a solution to this dilemma, both pointed at 'the human touch' (人情味), upon which they based their definitions of Taiwaneseness. Unlike the official 'Heart of Asia' campaign that only mentions the 'human factor', these designers' works develop this topic through a multitude of emotionally close, familiar elements related to personal life and memories. The following part will discuss three interrelated strategies they employ in both tourist souvenirs and other kinds of Taiwan-related works.[6]

Edensor (2002) speaks of everyday practices, mundane sights and objects recurrent across the nation, which shape a sense of national identity centred on a specific lifestyle. The first strategy consists in de-naturalising these usually 'unwaved, unsaluted and unnoticed … mindless flags' (Billig 1995: 40) hidden in the banal routines of everyday life, and making them visible as Taiwan's specificity (Figure 3). Ben spoke at length of his wish to go beyond typical tourist attractions in his souvenirs and 'dig down towards the roots' defined as objects and practices always present in everyday life: 'We found out that it's those things we're most accustomed to that may be among Taiwan's local characteristics'; 'things we come across every day in our life', 'something you use every day and can get at any general store'. Ariel also pointed out the everyday stories embodying Taiwaneseness: 'I often go and watch those very normal citizens. I like watching people in 7–11, old people with their Filipina maids. My life is full of stories that I could draw endlessly'. This strategy of turning Taiwan's mundaneness, even ugliness, into an extraordinary spectacle for the tourist gaze, allows the designers to create a national image that contrasts with the high-brow Chinese literati or imperial culture employed in identity discourses formulated by the KMT.

[6]Although the analysis below focuses only on works by the interviewed artists, they also apply to souvenirs by other designers (Zemanek 2017).

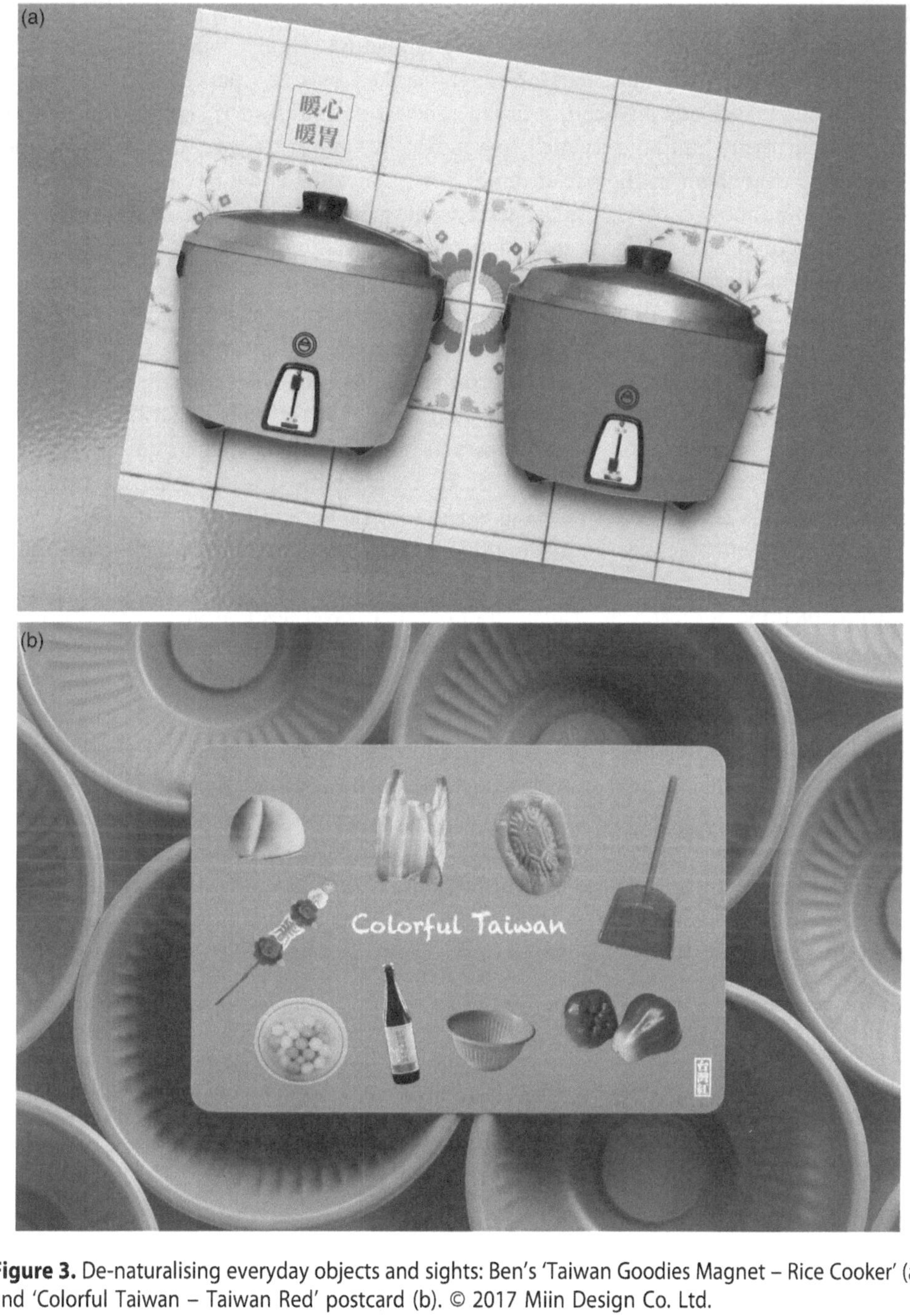

Figure 3. De-naturalising everyday objects and sights: Ben's 'Taiwan Goodies Magnet – Rice Cooker' (a) and 'Colorful Taiwan – Taiwan Red' postcard (b). © 2017 Miin Design Co. Ltd.

Ariel focuses on urban sights from Taipei. His souvenir series features living quarters seen from above as they have developed over the years, with roofs crowded into each other, of various sizes due to added illegal extensions covered with iron sheets, pigeon cages, small temples or gardens. The realistic drawings emphasise the haphazard character of such areas through minute details of laundry hung out to dry, odd objects stored on balconies, iron bars in windows, metal water reservoirs, TV aerials or air conditioners. Ariel's other works also depict vernacular architecture: similar buildings with street traffic below; street food stalls; narrow streets flanked by trees, parked cars and traffic signs. His newspaper ads advocating urban renewal combine such sights with modern high-rise apartment buildings (which, paradoxically, are to replace them[7]), or Taipei 101 towering over them in the background. Ben's souvenirs show city streets with busy traffic, the ubiquitous scooters, night market scenes with close-ups of food stalls and customers seated on plastic stools, or shop signs. Many depict individual objects to be found in the streets, in shops, restaurants, temples or homes all across Taiwan: plastic shopping bags, brooms, cooking utensils, human-sized traffic-directing dolls, or mail boxes. Frog's photograph postcards show various locations pinpointed on Taiwan's map placed on the reverse. They depict natural sceneries or ordinary sights: rice fields, ducklings in a pond, fish drying on wooden racks, or plastic flip-flops sold at street stalls. His video advertisement for a local recording company portrays Taiwan in everyday sights and sounds – a paddyfield in a sunny day with singing cicadas; city traffic around a flyover bridge; a small restaurant with customers chatting at outdoor tables and food stir-fried in a wok; an MRT station with the alert of closing doors and a view from inside with the sound of the train moving over the rails.

Such depictions of ordinariness instead of popular travel destinations or conventional images of history, modernity, 'traditional' culture or nature may reflect a worldwide, post-modern anti-auratic trend (Urry and Larsen 2011: 102–4). They may also overlap with an already existing Taiwan-related tourist gaze. Ben borrowed the themes of scooters, night markets and betelnut beauties from Western tour guides, and the Tatung rice cooker – from observations of Japanese tourists' consumer behaviour. However, these designers also bring forward new elements based on their own perceptions of Taiwaneseness as grounded in shared everyday practices specific to their national community. Ariel underscored his own interests as sole source of inspiration for his works. Ben emphasised his role in de-naturalising the everyday environment and expanding the gaze to areas unavailable to the usual tourist:

> At the beginning, we chose our topics according to those Taiwanese things that foreigners were interested in. After one or two years, we thought that we could actually start doing what we liked, too, and propose that to foreigners. What we like and what foreigners like don't always overlap. For instance, that series with the cow-shaped iron plate and the chopstick basket – those are things well-known to the Taiwanese, … things you would see while living in Taiwan, you wouldn't see them if you don't live here. If you're a tourist, you'd forget about them immediately, and you won't find them in tourist guides.

Following the de-naturalisation of everyday life, the second strategy is that of employing immediate, individual, bodily experiences for epistemological and representational processes involving both designers and audiences. Frog's postcards and video ads record his personal travels, and convey those experiences to the audience through compelling images and everyday sounds. His wooden souvenirs (glass coasters with indented regional maps, or Taiwan's map made up of puzzle pieces) invite purchasers' participation in an epistemological game involving their sense of touch. Ariel's rooftop series resulted

[7]For a more detailed critical stance on Ariel's contradictory behaviour related to Taipei's vernacular architecture and its representations, see Zemanek (forthcoming).

from personal observations from windows in his parents' house; his drawings for community-building events represent actual scenes, and are based on thorough knowledge of the environment: 'Because I know where I live, this is my home, so I'm very clear about every single blade of grass and tree growing there'. This sense of authenticity triggered recognition and emotional response from a local audience – elderly people who identified with the life stories and living spaces in his newspaper ads. Ben's souvenirs represent objects facilitating personal-level social contact: 'snacks are sold by street peddlers, the owner would get [to interact] face-to-face with the customers, so I think that this is where Taiwan lies'. Many are three-dimensional; they can function as substitutes for real-life objects and facilitate re-enacting Taiwan-related experiences (Figure 4). Ben's multi-purpose cards made of thick cardboard imitate animal-shaped cakes sold at street stalls. They are cut in actual cake shapes and come with a brown envelope copying actual packaging. A pair of bookmarks accurately reproduces blue-and-white plastic slippers. Two-sided refrigerator magnets imitate wooden moon blocks in temples and (as Ben pointed out) can be used for actual divination. Some postcards require the purchaser's participation in representing and re-experiencing Taiwan. By unfolding a paper lantern attached to a postcard, its addressee reproduces what people actually do before setting lighted lanterns into the sky. This strategy not only constructs a tourist gaze grounded in bodily practices, but also enables performances of national identity outside Taiwan. Ben reported that Taiwanese studying abroad regard his souvenirs as embodying a national specificity and offer them as gifts, use them for introducing Taiwanese culture, or sell them at university fairs.

The third strategy consists in constructing a vision of history grounded in personal experience and memories, which contrasts with China-centred nationalist discourses highlighting millennia-old traditions. Instead of focusing on 'cultural memory', i.e., 'fateful events of the past', stabilised and made accessible across centuries 'through cultural formation (texts, rites, monuments) and institutional communication (recitation, practice, observance)' (Assmann and Czaplicka 1995: 129), these designers turn towards 'everyday memory' and its limited temporal horizon based on individual experience and communication (127). Such an approach to history does not exclude more remote periods. Instead, it integrates them into the present through their material vestiges (such as the above-mentioned moon blocks originating in China), which are readily accessible in an everyday environment.

> 'We hope that our products will emphasise that we are Taiwanese. The objects we depict are essential elements of our life. Maybe some of them, culture or religion, came from China, but in fact many of our things are mixed, they also contain elements of Japanese culture. Just like the *kanban* [shop signs, a bookmark set theme] I mentioned before – this name is actually a Japanese word which entered Hokkien' (Ben, interview).

Ben and Ariel employ the human lifespan as unit for defining Taiwaneseness. Notwithstanding their origin, various objects or sights are Taiwanese due to their uninterrupted presence throughout an individual process of growing up, which makes them part of personal memories: 'this is the Taiwan I grew up in'; '[of rotating two-coloured columns in front of hair salons] Well, I don't know if they came from Japan, but such things were here when I was a child, so we turned them into [souvenir] products' (Ben); 'actually my motivation was not promoting Taiwan, I was only recording my memories from

Figure 4. Sensorial appeal and individual experience: Ben's '2D-Scene Postcard – Scooters on the Streets' (a) and 'Sponge Cake Card' set (b). © 2017 Miin Design Co. Ltd.

when I was growing up' (Ariel). Ariel's choice of ordinary living quarters as topics for his works is motivated by the vernacular, community-binding history they embody. This short-term, social history differs from the concept involved in state-led heritage preservation:

> Memory as I understand it is weak, their memory is antique, old, old architecture. My memory is of a rather social kind. [Such places are] natural! They're not artificial, not man-made, they're not that intentional, not as anyone wishes them to be. The government says, wow, that thing has four hundred years of history, we've got to protect it. What I draw is of the common people, it's not lofty, not that classic, you see it in ordinary life. My value is memory and nothing more, because everybody knows these memories.

This centrality of 'everyday memory' may be caused by distrust towards state-mediated knowledge. During my interviews, Frog markedly emphasised personal experience as epistemological method and expressed an aversion for books and school subjects: 'Many history books we used to read are all fake, they're not correct, we were inculcated with other histories'. Instead, he employs stories of actual, individual people to represent Taiwan.

8. Conclusions

According to critical scholars, nation branding serves elite interests and goes against the principles of plurality and democracy by excluding alternative narratives, limiting grassroots participation and failing to secure public consensus at home. My case studies suggest that these statements are not fully applicable to Taiwan. A constant 'state of inadequacy' makes Taiwan resemble Central and East European countries. It influences state actions and public diplomacy, but also has significant and manifold social reverberations. However, its key reason is not political, economic and social transition, but Taiwan's ambiguous status as sovereign nation. A strong, widespread imperative of formulating a 'desired identity' underlies both official and grassroots actors' branding efforts. The latter's personal stake in branding the nation reflects an individual quest for national identity.

Despite this common goal, the interviewed designers markedly position themselves outside the state. This can be explained by scepticism towards party politics and the government, an attitude widespread in Taiwan and also observed in Romania (Bardan and Imre 2012). However, their relationship with the state cannot be described as simple antagonism. Unlike the Polish 'new cultural intermediaries', whose desire for prestige causes complicity with state branding efforts (Surowiec 2012), my interviewees reject this kind of symbolic capital and persist in promoting their own definitions of Taiwaneseness, apparently notwithstanding their lack of economic profitability. They criticise official policies regarding the cultural and creative industries as conducive to excessive commercialisation. But it is these policies, combined with the pervasive official and popular interest in defining Taiwan, which have created prestige and economic feasibility for their activities. Ben can support less profitable souvenirs with revenue from more successful ones. Ariel makes up for setbacks in selling souvenirs with other kinds of commissioned projects, and by 'smuggling' similar images into more profitable products (newspaper ads). Frog skilfully combines his Taiwan-branding activity with new business and tourism models shaped by the development of the cultural and creative industries and a general demand for definitions of Taiwan on the local market. As he stated in a 2016 magazine article, '"Taiwan" is a topic that's really worth taking up' (「台灣」可以是一項值得經營的項目).

These designers' messages have less international impact than official branding campaigns. They only target small audiences (specific groups of foreign tourists) instead of a community of nation-states, and are not present on internationally authoritative platforms such as the Tourism Bureau website. However, unlike the state, they create an 'intertextual environment of citation and implication' through 'multiple, sequenced interventions' (Graan 2016: 86) ensuring reproduction and reinforcement of their Taiwan-related discourses for both a local and a foreign public. Although unrelated, these designers' images of Taiwan overlap. Moreover, apart from traditional souvenir sales channels, they actively develop alternative, highly efficient marketing networks with local individuals and institutions such as media outlets, Taiwanese students abroad, NGOs, companies or government organisations commissioning design projects. Motivated by various affinities with my interviewees' activity, these agents increase the circulation of their messages (expressed through souvenirs and in other forms). Their activity also intersects with state-endorsed issues: cycling, traditional culture or community-building.

In Taiwan, the state as nation branding actor is constrained by 'political palace struggling', highlighted by Kaneva (2012) in an East European context and confirmed by Rawnsley (2014). The necessity to avoid sensitive issues susceptible to challenging the cross-strait status quo results in images that incorporate rather than replace the previously hegemonic China-centred identity. The 'Heart of Asia' campaign imports the Western 'nation branding gospel' by outsourcing its visual design, a probable reason for its generalised, clichéd quality. By contrast, grassroots actors can freely decide on subject matters and styles. Far from displaying the Central and East European 'West complex', they draw inspiration from foreign sources, but develop their own, coherent identification for Taiwan and a unique tourist gaze based on 'the human touch' through the following strategies: de-naturalisation of everyday sights and objects; a personal, sensorial involvement in knowing, representing and re-enacting Taiwan; a vernacular view of history with the human lifespan as basic temporal unit, which draws attention to everyday social interaction and makes history available through material vestiges present in ordinary living spaces. As the 'human touch' theme is present in official materials, such definitions of Taiwan do not counteract, but complement the state campaign. Nevertheless, their persuasive potential is higher. As a category, familiar objects and spaces reproduced on souvenirs are likely to strike an emotional chord with foreign addressees. Additionally, they trigger instant recognition from local audiences.

Regardless of changes in ruling parties, the state in post-martial law era Taiwan does not suppress alternative national narratives. However, it fails to involve grassroots actors as active, prominent partners in major branding projects and seems to largely ignore their efforts. The evolution of official cultural policies may cause their messages to ultimately converge. Nevertheless, joining forces may prove to be a difficult task requiring a high degree of openness, flexibility and trust.

Acknowledgements

I would like to thank Teri Silvio for encouraging me to contribute to this special issue, and for inviting me to present an earlier version of my study at the Academia Sinica Institute of Ethnology. I also thank the audience (and especially A-chin Hsiau) for the questions and comments raised after my presentation, and the two anonymous reviewers for their valuable feedback. All these suggestions have greatly contributed to improving this paper.

Disclosure statement

No potential conflict of interest was reported by the author.

References

Aronczyk, M. 2009. 'How to Do Things with Brands: Uses of National Identity'. *Canadian Journal of Communication* 34, 291–96.

Aronczyk, M. 2013. *Branding the Nation: The Global Business of National Identity*. Oxford and New York: Oxford University Press.

Assmann, J. and Czaplicka, J. 1995. 'Collective Memory and Cultural Identity'. *New German Critique* 65, 125–33.

Bardan, A. and Imre, A. 2012. 'Vampire Branding. Romania's Dark Destinations'. In Nadia Kaneva (ed), *Branding Post-Communist Nations: Marketizing National Identities in the "New" Europe*. New York and London: Routledge, 168–92.

Berger, S., Eriksonas, L. and Mycock, A. 2008. *Narrating the Nation. Representations in History, Media and the Arts*. New York and Oxford: Berghahn Books.

Billig, M. 1995. *Banal Nationalism*. London, Thousand Oaks and New Delhi: SAGE Publications.

Chang, B. 2006. 'Constructing the Motherland: Culture and the State Since the 1990s'. In Dafydd Fell, Henning Klöter, and Chang Bi-yu (eds), *What Has Changed? Taiwan Before and After the Change in Ruling Parties*. Wiesbaden: Harrassowitz Verlag, 187–206.

Chen, K. 2010. *Asia as Method. Toward Deimperialization*. Durham and London: Duke University Press.

Chen, C. 2014. 'Suitable Festival Activities for Taiwan's Tourism and Nation Branding with the Application of the PR AHP Program'. *Asia Pacific Journal of Tourism Research* 19:12, 1381–98.

Dinnie, K. 2008. *Nation Branding. Concepts, Issues, Practice*. Amsterdam, London and New York: Elsevier.

Edensor, T. 2002. *National Identity, Popular Culture and Everyday Life*. Oxford and New York: Berg.

Graan, A. 2016. 'The Nation Brand Regime: Nation Branding and the Semiotic Regimentation of Public Communication in Contemporary Macedonia'. *Signs and Society* 4:S1, S70–S105.

Harrison, M. 2009. 'How to Speak About Oneself. Theory and Identity in Taiwan'. In Chris Berry, Nicola Liscutin, and Jonathan D. Mackintosh (eds), *Cultural Studies and Cultural Industries in Northeast Asia. What a Difference a Region Makes*. Hong Kong: Hong Kong University Press, 51–70.

Harrison, M. 2015. 'Art, Violence and Memory: Retelling the Story of the Beautiful Island'. Keynote speech presented at the conference 'Taiwan: The View from the South', Canberra, January 9, 2015. Available online at http://ciw.anu.edu.au/events/2015/taiwanconference/ (accessed 14 December 2016).

Ho, M. 2014. 'The Resurgence of Social Movements Under the Ma Ying-jeou Government'. In Jean-Pierre Cabestan and Jacques deLisle (eds), *Political Changes in Taiwan Under Ma Ying-jeou. Partisan Conflict, Policy Choices, External Constraints and Security Challenges*. Abingdon and New York: Routledge, 100–19.

Hsiau, A. 2012. 'Zhuiqiu minzu: 1980 niandai Taiwan minzuzhuyi de wenhua zhengzhi' (追求民族: 1980年代台灣民族主義的文化政治) [Searching for the Nation: The Cultural Politics of Taiwanese Nationalism in the 1980s]. *Reflexions* 22, 85–110.

Hughes, C. 2014. 'Revisiting Identity Politics Under Ma Ying-jeou'. In Jean-Pierre Cabestan and Jacques deLisle (eds), *Political Changes in Taiwan Under Ma Ying-jeou. Partisan Conflict, Policy Choices, External Constraints and Security Challenges*. Abingdon and New York: Routledge, 121–36.

Kaneva, N. 2012. 'Nation Branding in Post-Communist Europe. Identities, Markets, and Democracy'. In Nadia Kaneva (ed), *Branding Post-Communist Nations: Marketizing National Identities in the "New" Europe*. New York and London: Routledge, 3–22.

Liao, R. 2014. 'Ningshi Taiwan, xiehou aiqing: cong weidianying xushi fangshi kan lüyou yixiang de meiti zaixian' (凝視臺灣, 邂逅愛情: 從微電影敘事方式看旅遊意象的媒體再現) [Gazing Taiwan, Meeting Love: Exploring Media Representations of Tourist Image in Microfilm Narrative]. Available online at http://ccs.nccu.edu.tw/paperdetail.asp?HP_ID=1600 (accessed 17 April 2017).

Lu, H. 2002. *The Politics of Locality. Making a Nation of Communities in Taiwan*. New York and London: Routledge.

Pamment, J. 2015. 'Putting the GREAT Back Into Britain: National Identity, Public-Private Collaboration & Transfers of Brand Equity in 2012s Global Promotional Campaign'. *The British Journal of Politics and International Relations* 17, 260–83.

Phillips, N. and Hardy, C. 2002. *Discourse Analysis. Investigating Processes of Social Construction*. Thousand Oaks and London: SAGE.

Rawnsley, G. 2014. 'Taiwan's Soft Power and Public Diplomacy'. *Journal of Current Chinese Affairs* 43:3, 161–74.

Saunders, R. A. 2012. 'Brand Interrupted. The Impact of Alternative Narrators on Nation Branding in the Former Second World'. In Nadia Kaneva (ed), *Branding Post-Communist Nations: Marketizing National Identities in the "New" Europe*. New York and London: Routledge, 49–75.

Sturken, M. 1997. *Tangled Memories: The Vietnam War, the AIDS Epidemic, and the Politics of Remembering*. Berkeley: University of California Press.

Surowiec, P. 2012. 'Toward Corpo-Nationalism. Poland as a Brand'. In Nadia Kaneva (ed), *Branding Post-Communist Nations: Marketizing National Identities in the "New" Europe*. New York and London: Routledge, 124–44.

Taylor, J. E. 2010. '*Qujianghua*: Disposing of and Re-Appraising the Remnants of Chiang Kai-Shek's Reign on Taiwan'. *Journal of Contemporary History* 45:1, 181–96.

Tsai, I. 2015. 'Hou zhi wenhua li, dazao Taiwan wenyi fuxing xin shidai' (厚植文化力, 打造台灣文藝復興新時代) [Firmly Establishing the Strength of Culture, Forging a New Era of Taiwanese Renaissance]. Available online at http://iing.tw/posts/200 (accessed 28 March 2017).

Urry, J. and Larsen, J. 2011. *The Tourist Gaze 3.0*. Los Angeles and London: SAGE.

Wodak, R. 2001. 'The Discourse-Historical Approach'. In Ruth Wodak and Michael Meyer (eds), *What CDA is About – A Summary of its History, Important Concepts and Its Developments*. London: SAGE Publications, 63–94.

You, Y. 2013. Yi wenhua chuangyi chanye guannian kaifa Jiayi nongchang zhi kexingxing yanjiu (以文化創意產業觀念開發嘉義農場之可行性研究) [Feasibility Assessment of Chiayi Farming Development According to Principles of Cultural and Creative Industries]. MA dissertation, National Cheng Kung University.

Zemanek, A. 2017. 'Familiar Spaces: (National) Home in Contemporary Taiwanese Tourist Souvenirs'. *China Perspectives* 2, 7–17.

Zemanek, A. forthcoming. 'Getting to Know Taiwan: Borrowed Gaze, Direct Involvement and Everyday Life'. Chapter submitted for Bi-yu Chang and Pei-yin Lin (eds), *Taiwan Imagined: Global Gaze, Local Negotiation, and Identity Formation*, ongoing book project.

Zhang, G. and Wang, Y. 2000. 'You guojijian guojia pinpai fazhan guiji, fajue Taiwan dute xiyinli' (由國際間國家品牌發展軌跡, 發掘台灣獨特吸引力) [Exploring Taiwan's Distinctive Attractiveness from the Perspective of International Paths in Brand Developing]. *Taiwan Economic Research Monthly* 33:2, 40–48.

5 Representing creative labour and identity in Singaporean graphic novels: Sonny Liew and Troy Chin

Teri Silvio

ABSTRACT

This essay analyses two Singaporean graphic novels which represent the motivations and processes of creating and marketing cartoons, Sonny Liew's *The Art of Charlie Chan Hock Chye* (2015), a retrospective of the life and work of a fictional artist, and Troy Chin's ongoing autobiographical series, *The Resident Tourist* (begun in 2007). The analysis focuses on how Liew and Chin represent creative work and its relationship to Singaporean identity, focusing on how each negotiates one of the central contradictions of the creative industries in Singapore, the problem of how creativity can be conceptualised and practised within a society in which, for decades, pragmatism has been systematically valued and imagination devalued. There are three main ways in which both Liew and Chin construct, in very different ways, new creative worker and Singaporean identities which resonate with readers around the post-industrial world. The first is through subtle challenges to the Western, individualised 'genius' model of the creative worker. The second is through the creation of modes of address that encompass both Singaporean and non-Singaporean readers, and make all readers complicit in the project of constructing Singaporean identity. Third, both Liew and Chin reimagine the relationship between Singaporean and creative worker identities through simultaneously using and subverting the idea of national allegory.

Like the governments of many Asian countries after the financial crisis of 1997–1998, Singapore's ruling People's Action Party (PAP) felt the need to begin restructuring the economy to adjust to global transformations that were clearly underway. With international investors moving from Singapore to China for manufacturing, the PAP instituted a wide range of policies aimed at transforming the island into a global centre of the creative economy. In their planning to transform Singapore into a 'Renaissance City' and a 'Global City for the Arts', the PAP studied and adapted discourses and strategies for developing a creative economy from many other countries, particularly the US and the UK, but also Finland, Spain, Australia, Hong Kong, and South Korea. As Kong, et al. point out, Singaporean

> policy-makers do not hesitate to reference circulating discourses, particularly by 'popular' academic authors like Richard Florida and John Howkins. Engagement with these discourses

> is, however, not especially profound, lingering mainly at the level of offering justification rather than deep engagement with specific ideas ... All of these specific lessons from travelling discourses contribute to the more general narratives that permeate policy documents. (2006: 179)

This includes promoting 'creativity and culture as a means to place competition, improving the quality of life to attract foreign talent, thus enhancing national competitiveness' (2006: 179).

Despite the relative ease with which global creative industries discourse, and policies such as building infrastructure, boosting arts education, and importing foreign talent, fit into the PAP's existing framework, the development of the creative industries in Singapore appears to be a problematic, if not outright contradictory endeavour, not only to foreign observers, but to many Singaporean creative workers themselves. Contradictions between the global discourse and practices of creative industry development and local conditions exist in many countries. In Singapore's case, the problem arises from the PAP's longstanding ideology, which Audrey Yue (2012) calls 'illiberal pragmatism'. Since the 1960s, the PAP has promoted a 'vigorous economic development orientation that emphasizes science and technology and centralized rational public administration ... financed largely by multinational capital' (Chua 1995: 59), and policies which intervene into many aspects of citizens' daily lives, sometimes changing and contradictory, are consistently justified in utilitarian terms.

Many scholars studying the arts and creative industries in Singapore have focused on the 'illiberal' aspect of 'illiberal pragmatism', in particular noting the clash between Richard Florida's thesis that the development of creative industries requires a vibrant, open, and tolerant cultural scene and the PAP's regulation of many aspects of citizens' behaviour and expression, particularly the strict censorship of sensitive content (e.g., Lim 1997, Smith 2016). This conflict was even noted in the Media Development Authority's 2002 proposal, *Creative Industries Development Strategy: Propelling Singapore's Creative Economy*, in which one of Singapore's weaknesses was assessed in this way:

> Singapore needs to shake off its image of being an 'over-regulated' city state, with a low tolerance for divergent views. Creative people and enterprises are attracted to, and flourish in places which are tolerant of creative discourse and provide space for experimentation. (Media Development Authority 2002: 7)

For those trying to develop the Singaporean creative industries from within, however, the ideology of pragmatism poses a deeper set of problems than illiberalism. What Aihwa Ong says of the development of the Singaporean knowledge economy applies to the creative economy as well: 'at stake ... is the reorganization of society and of citizens' (2006: 179); the development of the creative economy means changing cultural values; it involves transforming Singaporean national identity at its core.

For decades, Singaporean identity has been constructed in opposition to both culture and creativity. While Singapore sells itself as a multicultural, cosmopolitan metropolis, Singaporean national identity has been built on the transcendence, rather than the blending, of ethnic cultures. And this transcendence, in turn, has been built on a concept of pragmatism which, by definition, excludes that which is 'irrational' or 'useless'. Until the turn toward the creative economy, art was seen as a distraction from the work of nation-building; Lee Kwan Yew famously remarked in 1968 that 'Poetry is a luxury we cannot afford'. Thus the development of a creative economy in Singapore presents the problem of what the PAP often refers to as 'mind-set'. As Wan-Ling Wee puts it:

> [H]eavy state intervention since the 1960s has produced, ironically, a passive (and thus successfully homogenized) population that may not have the necessary cultural dynamism to propel the city-state to be a player in the supposedly more freewheeling and less-Fordist New or Creative Economy that marked the closing decade of the twentieth century. (2007: 90)

The transformation of the economy entails transformations in Singapore's relation to the world, and in what it means to be Singaporean. From the outside, the conflict inherent in the development of Singapore's creative industries appears to be one between artists' self-expression and the state. From the inside, however, the conflict is often experienced most sharply before any self-expression takes place. It is a conflict, at both the societal and individual level, between different moral economies and between past and future identities.

The tension between old and new values is not only manifest in the content produced by Singaporean creative workers, but in how they manage their careers within an emerging gig economy. This may be particularly true of comics artists, who lack the corporate infrastructure and the possibility of long-term jobs available to creative workers in other fields such as advertising or television production. In this essay, I want to look at how two graphic novelists, Sonny Liew and Troy Chin, represent and meet the challenges of creative labour in contemporary Singapore. I will do this by analysing their two best-known works, both of which are meta-comics, that is, graphic novels that are about the work of creating comics – Liew's *The Art of Charlie Chan Hock Chye* and Chin's *The Resident Tourist* series.

Both Liew and Chin are award-winning artists with fans around the world. They are not typical of Singaporean comics artists – this is a very small group, which is so diverse that it would be impossible to find a 'typical' artist. But I believe their success is at least in part due to the solutions they have found for dealing with the contradictions of creative work in Singapore. Both artists represent Singapore simultaneously as a particular place with a unique history, and as an instantiation of global neoliberal conditions, and both have created new possibilities for Singaporean and creative worker identities.

Before I begin textual and visual analysis of *The Art of Charlie Chan* and *The Resident Tourist*, let me give some background on the particular place of comics within the Singaporean creative industries.

Labour conditions for comics artists in Singapore

The Media Development Authority (MDA) divides the creative industries into three sectors: arts and culture, design, and media. Graphic novelists are categorised by the Singapore government as part of the arts and culture sector, which includes the visual and literary arts. Comics are marginal even within the publishing industry, and comic book production does not yet constitute an industry in itself. As Troy Chin put it in a recent interview (E-Quill Media 2017a),

> The comic book industry in Singapore is pretty much non-existent right now, because I'm very strict when it comes to the definition of an industry. Do we have a scene? Maybe, because there seem to be circles of folks who are doing zines, and they show up at meets

> once in a while. So there is sort of a scene. But as far as the industry is concerned, we don't have one yet. Because for an industry to exist, there needs to be an ecosystem where people can come together, get paid for their work, have a legit contract, have publishers who are willing to sign them readily, maybe even agents or editors involved ... But right now, as far as Singapore is concerned, we're still at baby steps, everything has to be grassroots, everything has to be initiated by the person themselves ... The situation has changed over the last ten years ... now publishers are more willing to put [comic] books out.

For original comics artists in Singapore, some of the most salient conditions are the same as those in most places outside of the US, Japan, and France, the countries with the largest comics industries. Certain genres in which comics artists may work have histories going back to the British colonial era or earlier. These include newspaper cartoons, including both political and light humour, as well as children's entertainment and educational comic books (Singapore's educational comics sell quite well both domestically and internationally). However, the Singaporean comic book market is dominated by American comics, particularly Marvel and DC Comics' superhero series, with Japanese manga (imported mostly in Chinese, from Taiwan) following closely behind. Artists and publishers are well aware that the local market is simply not large enough to sustain a local industry on its own.

As comics scholars note, it is almost impossible to make a living solely as an original comics artist in Singapore. A few artists get contracts with comics publishers in the US or Japan, and a few are able to draw comics almost full time because they are independently wealthy. However, for the majority of Singaporean artists, comics are a side project done in their spare time. Most depend for a living on other work, such as freelance graphic design, advertising, and teaching (Lim 2014; Lent 2015; Smith 2016).

The internet provides a major space for amateur comics artists, both for secondary works (that is, fan manga using characters from existing commercial franchises) and original works. Many young artists practise their craft and try to build an audience by posting their work on personal blogs.

For artists who have completed a graphic novel and wish to publish and market it in Singapore, however, there are only a few options. Since the mid-2000s, the government has provided grants, through the MDA, the National Book Development Council, and the National Arts Council (NAC), for the development and publication of graphic novels, although these are rare. There are also a few entrepreneurs in Singapore who actively support the production and marketing of literary graphic novels by local artists despite the fact that the market is too small to make a profit. Edmund Wee, founder of Epigram Books, has sought out literary works (including poetry, novels, and plays) by local authors with local content to publish, and the publishing is largely funded through his design firm. Epigram Books began a series of local graphic novels in 2011, with a grant from the MDA, and has published 13 so far.[1] Kenny Leck is the founder of BooksActually, a bookstore that regularly hosts events such as author readings and pop-up stores throughout the city. Leck also started a boutique press, Math Paper Press, in 2011, which publishes graphic novels as well as poetry, novels, and plays. Local comics artist Wee Tian Beng established TCZ Studio in 2011, which produces educational comics plus a few original series by local artists in globalised popular genres,

[1] Interview with author, September 2015.

including Wee's own *Celestial Zone* martial arts fantasy series. Other artists turn to overseas publishers. The careers of Liew and Chin are illustrative of the complex negotiations that Singaporean comics artists make between government sponsorship and the gig economy, between local and overseas publishers and markets.

Some of these negotiations are represented directly in Chin's autobiographical *The Resident Tourist* series, for instance when he expresses his ambivalence about taking an NAC grant or narrates his conversations with his agent in Thailand. The formal qualities of both *The Resident Tourist* and *The Art of Charlie Chan* are also shaped by these negotiations, and are in fact themselves strategies in these negotiations.

In the following analysis, I want to argue that there are three main ways in which both Liew and Chin have constructed new creative worker and Singaporean identities through their comics, identities which seem to resonate with readers around the post-industrial world. First, both artists provide visions of the function of art and the nature of the creative process that challenge those of the Singapore government's discourse and the international creative industry theorists on whom it draws. Second, they construct modes of address that encompass both Singaporean and non-Singaporean readers, and make all readers complicit in the project of constructing Singaporean identity. Third, both Liew and Chin reimagine the relationship between Singaporean and creative worker identities through simultaneously using and subverting the idea of national allegory.

Sonny Liew and *The Art of Charlie Chan Hock Chye*

Sonny Liew was born in 1974 In Malaysia, but moved to Singapore as a child. He studied Philosophy at Cambridge and then illustration at the Rhode Island School of Design. He moved back to Singapore in 2002. Liew works in several venues, including newspaper strips, anthologies and full-length graphic novels, and he has received several international prizes. He has worked as a writer and artist for Marvel, DC Comics and Disney, and this, along with freelance illustration, is his main source of income.

Liew is one of the major figures in the Singapore comics scene, in the role of both artist and editor. Before *The Art of Charlie Chan*, he published a full-colour science fiction comic, *Malinky Robot* (2011), set in a dystopian near-future Asian city, and edited three anthologies of Southeast Asian local comics' short pieces, *Liquid City* Volumes 1–3 (2008, 2010, 2014). Both *Malinky Robot* and *Liquid City* were published by Image Comics, Inc., based in Berkeley, California.[2] He also illustrated the Asian-American superhero comic, *The Shadow Hero*, written by award-winning American artist Gene Luen Yang (2014, published by First Second, New York).

The Art of Charlie Chan Hock Chye takes the form of an art book retrospective of the work and life of a fictional Singaporean comics artist. The book compiles a variety of different genres and styles, including comics by the eponymous Charlie Chan in different genres, reproductions of his childhood drawings, paintings, and unfinished works, interviews with him (represented in the form of comics), and comments by a cartoon representation of Sonny Liew himself. We are presented with the history of Singapore from the 1940s to the present, moving back and forth between daily life (in Charlie's relatively realist autobiographical comics and the interview pages) and major political events.

[2]Volume 2 of *Liquid City* was co-edited with Lim Cheng Tju; Volume 3 was co-edited with Joyce Sim.

Much of the book focuses on the real historical figures of Lee Kuan Yew, founder of the PAP and Prime Minister of Singapore for 31 years, and Lim Chin Siong, Lee's sometime ally, sometime rival, founder of the leftist Barisan Sosialis party. Lim was accused of being a Communist and twice detained without trial, from 1956–1959 and from 1963–1969, after which he spent the rest of his life in exile in London. The bare historical facts about these two characters are given in commentaries by the Sonny character and through reproduced newspaper clippings, and documented in detail in the footnotes.[3] But the overall approach history in *The Art of Charlie Chan* is classically post-modernist – different versions of every historical event are juxtaposed, every narrator is revealed as unreliable, and Liew is almost obsessively reflexive about the impossibility of representing historical truth. Liew claims that his main purpose in creating the comic was not to present 'a revisionist history as much as a more inclusive one' (Guimaraes n.d.), and it has been compared to Art Spiegelman's *Maus* and Marjane Satrapi's *Persepolis*.

The Art of Charlie Chan Hock Chye was published in 2015 by Epigram, and then licensed to Pantheon for distribution globally in 2016. Liew received an NAC grant for 8,000 SGD to create the book, but the grant was rescinded after the book was printed. The official reason for rescinding the grant from the NAC was that 'The retelling of Singapore's history in the work potentially undermines the authority or legitimacy of the Government and its public institutions, and thus breaches our funding guidelines' (Han 2015). News of the de-granting actually gave Liew free publicity. The book sold out and went into a second printing within days of its launch. In 2017, it won three Eisner awards, making Liew the first Singaporean artist to win the most prestigious international award for comics art.

The Art of Charlie Chan contains tropes for the nation at several intertwined levels. First, there is the 'life and times' aspect of the narrative, in which Charlie serves as a synecdoche for ordinary Singaporeans who lived through all the dramatic political, economic and social upheavals of the 1940s to 1980s. Charlie's parents own a neighbourhood sundries store, he attends an English language school, and his career is easily affected by economic depressions. He is barely able to meet the obligation to care for his aging parents, and achieves fame and fortune only in his fantasies. Like the vast majority of citizens, he watches political events unfolding from a distance. This type of synecdochal life is quite common for protagonists in Singaporean graphic novels.

More striking is the use of explicit allegory in the majority of the comics-within-the-comic. These include 'Bukit Chapalang' (meaning 'Hodgepodge Hill' in Malay), modelled on Walt Kelly's *Pogo*, with Lee Kwan-yew as Sang Kancil, a mouse-deer (a trickster figure in Malay folklore) and Lim Chin Siong as a cat, and 'Sinkapor Inks', in which Lee appears as the director of a stationery supplies company. In 'Invasion!' a terminally ill boy, Tommy Tan, awakes from cryo-sleep in 2034 to discover that Singapore has been taken over by an alien race, the Hegemons. He joins the resistance, led by Lee Kuan Yew and Lim Chin Siong together. 'Days of August' is set in a future in which the Barisan Sosialis, instead of the PAP, won the 1963 elections. At the end of the comic, the cartoonist Charlie Chan, a national treasure with a museum dedicated to his work in this world, realises

[3]Following convention for discussing autobiographical narrative, I use last names (Liew and Chin) to refer to the artists as creators, and first names (Sonny and Troy) to refer to representations of the artists as characters within the works.

that this version of the future is just a fantasy, and is transported, along with Lim, back to 1955, to face a future in which they will inevitably 'fail'.

The 'life and times' synecdoche and the political allegories, and tensions between the public and private spheres and between art and commerce, are interwoven through parallel sets of characters and relationships, particularly parallels between Lee and Lim on the one hand and Charlie and his writing and business partner, Bertrand, on the other. As reviewer Kyle Pinion writes:

> Liew swings a particularly tough dramatic punch by the story's back-half, at the moment when Chan's partnership with writer Bertrand Wong comes to an end due to the need to find a 'practical vocation'. This dovetails with Lim and Lee's partnership dissolving and the mindset that Singapore found itself in during its post-failed Malaysian merger. At this point in time, the Lee Kuan Yew led government began to guide the newly independent nation with a strong hand, leading to economic growth but also crushing needed freedoms, such as Lee's need to overtake the press in an attempt to quell any personal or political causes that may speak out against the ruling regime. The question posed by Liew (vis a vis Chan) is one of 'what do we leave behind in order to gain material prosperity?' (Pinion 2016)

Charlie's comics are neither utopian nor dystopian, or perhaps they are both at once. The fantastic settings serve to create some distance between the viewer and the present, allowing for multiple visions of alternative futures to appear. Aimee Bahng (2015) has argued that Liew's earlier comic book, *Malinky Robot*, poses a challenge to the official neoliberal vision of 'Asian futurity', through stories of a human boy and his companion creature optimistically pursuing their dreams and creating a caring community in a future Asian city of decaying skyscrapers and toxic rivers. In *The Art of Charlie Chan*, the optimism does not come from any vision of a single alternative future in which Lim Chin Siong had become the leader of Singapore – even in 'Days of August', Lee Kwan Yew literally haunts the narrative. Rather, it comes from the imagining, consistent in Charlie's speculative fiction comics, of the re-incorporation of the repressed 'impractical' back into Singapore's identity.

Charlie's obsession with allegory may also be itself read as part of another level of synecdoche, in which Charlie, and by extension Liew, stand in for Singaporean creative workers generally. Charlie has much in common with many creative workers who operate outside of large industries throughout Asia. Like Liew, and most of the graphic novelists and illustrators I have interviewed in Taiwan, Hong Kong and Singapore, his interest in art goes back to his childhood; he begins with a love of comic books, and teaches himself by copying drawings from them. Unlike Liew, Charlie is entirely self-taught. Charlie is, in some sense, similar to the centuries-old European model of the artist, motivated by a sense of mission to create innovative and meaningful works, and stubbornly willing to sacrifice his material well-being to keep practising his craft.

But Charlie is not striving merely for self-expression, or to create art with 'universal' value. He specifically wants to create comics that will encourage political consciousness and a sense of identity for Singaporeans. Also, unlike the classical model of the creative worker, but more like the more contemporary model, Charlie sees the idea of unique genius, or the purely original artwork, as spurious. Like Liew, Charlie is a master of stylistic appropriation – both display their virtuosity through imitating the styles of other artists, including Osamu Tezuka, Walt Kelly, Carl Barks, Jack Kirby, Winsor McCay, Hergé and Harvey Kurtzman.

It is significant that Charlie is not based on any real Singaporean artist, or even a composite of actual historical Singaporean comics artists, but more a projection of Liew's own self-image into the past. The fact that Singaporean creative worker identity cannot grow out of Singapore's modern history, that it must be imagined from scratch, presents both limitations and possibilities for Liew. One limitation is that Charlie's orientation is the same as Liew's, that of an English-educated, ethnically Chinese Singaporean, and one which follows, in a general way, the history of the PAP's orientations from Britain to Japan and then to the US (Wee 2007). With the exception of Tezuka and one brief mention of the Hong Kong children's comics magazine *Ertong Leyuan*, all of the artists who are visually cited in *The Art of Charlie Chan* are North American or European – there are no stylistic references to other Asian comics that a reader of Charlie's generation might have come across, such as those by Malaysia's influential Lat, or Hong Kong's martial arts comics or *Master Q*, or India's English language Amar Chitra Katha mythological comics.

Rather than drawing on any historical Asian comics tradition, Liew creates a new one, while highlighting its status as invented tradition. At one point, Charlie claims that America's Spiderman character was an imitation of his sensationalist superhero, Roachman, a night-soil collector who gains superpowers when bitten by a cockroach (Figure 1). The claim seems to be of a piece with the fantasies of grandiosity which Charlie self-mockingly represents in a series of comics parodying McCay's 'Dreams of a Rarebit Fiend'. Yet Charlie's claim is not represented in one of his comics, but in an interview section, and although it seems at first absurd, given the fact that Walt Disney's influence on Tezuka was reciprocated in the Disney Company's later appropriation of Tezuka's *Simba* stories for *The Lion King* (Patten 2007), is not at all unimaginable. Liew thus points to the possibilities of alternative art histories as yet undiscovered. He presents us with a speculative, anti-colonialist history of comics art itself, one that is not meant to replace historical facts, but to suggest alternative futures.

It is through this mode of self-conscious invented tradition, of existing history as a resource for creating multiple alternative histories and futures, that Liew is able to create a new global public. Publics are constructed, as Warner (2002) notes, by address alone, and by the 'mere attention' of addressees. Here, Liew's starting from scratch approach works to his advantage. While *The Art of Charlie Chan* is clearly addressed to an English-fluent, intellectual audience, Liew assumes that both Singaporeans and non-Singaporeans are equally unfamiliar with the unofficial Singapore Story he relates, and with the history of comics art. The onslaught of facts and footnotes, which encourage readers to recreate Liew's own educational process, may put some readers off, which Liew understands. In keeping with his hyper-self-conscious and self-deprecating style, Liew even features an embedded strip at the bottom of some pages, in which a bored teen reacts to the Sonny character's manic history lessons by looking at his cellphone and saying 'Meh' (Figure 2). However, because this educational path is embedded in the text, Liew is also able to make interested readers complicit in the reconstruction of both Singaporean and creative worker identities, making a history of popular culture part of the deep structure of a new understanding of Singapore, and Singapore's history of political cooperations and separations, of the tension between political pragmatism and idealism, a trope for how global creative industries emerge.

Figure 1. Charlie's Roachman character (reproduced with permission of Sonny Liew and Epigram Books Pte Ltd.)

Figure 2. The Sonny character converses with a stand-in for the young Singaporean reader. (Reproduced with permission of Sonny Liew and Epigram Books Pte Ltd.)

Troy Chin's *The Resident Tourist* – problematising developmentalist trajectories of the self

Troy Chin was born in 1978 in Singapore, and left in 1998 for studies in the US. He graduated from the Wharton Business School and then worked in the music industry, as a financial executive for Sony-BGM in New York. In 2007, he quit that job and returned to Singapore to try making a living as a comics artist. For several years he lived with his mother and had virtually no income, focusing on drawing his comics. Once he had become known within arts circles, he was able to make a living from his comics as well as government grants, taking occasional illustration cases, lecturing, and teaching. He began publishing episodes of his best known work, *The Resident Tourist*, on his personal blog. He self-published the first five books. Since Part 6, the series has been published by Kenny Leck's Math Paper Press.[4] From 2008 to 2011, he also published a children's comic strip, 'Loti', on his blog, and later published it in a series of books. Chin continues to post drawings and comments, as well as audio mix tapes to accompany his comics, on his blog. In 2011, he won the NAC's Young Artist Award.

The Resident Tourist records Chin's experiences in New York and after returning home, and, as one character in Part 6 sums it up, 'combine[s] the visual style of manga with the alternative storytelling of the west'. The narrative skips back and forth between different times in Chin's life, from his present in Singapore, to his life in New York, to his elementary school days, to his two years of mandatory military service. This narrative is held together by an authorial voice that appears in captions. The series is reminiscent of several celebrated graphic novels from the US, especially those of Harvey Pekar (in its detailed observations of the daily lives of a variety of people, told in the first person) and Alison Bechdel (in that the series grew out of the process of psychotherapy, and is self-consciously a 'working-through'). Like *The Art of Charlie Chan*, it is a meta-comic which spends a great deal of time reflecting on the work of creating the comic itself.

Like Sonny Liew, Chin is interested in deconstructing the narratives that dominate Singaporean discourse, and in the question of what gets lost in the pragmatic pursuit of a good life defined in purely material terms. But unlike Liew, he does not do so through the postmodernist approach of presenting multiple perspectives on the grand narratives of politics and history. His approach is relentlessly realist, and he focuses on everyday life. He has said that his goal is 'the accurate depiction of Singapore life, and the modern Singaporean living

[4]Part 9 of *The Resident Tourist* was published by Math Paper Press in 2017, after I finished writing the first draft of this paper. The analysis here is limited to Parts 1 through 8 and the short piece in *Liquid City* Volume One (Chin 2008, 2009, 2010, 2011a, 2011b, 2011c, 2014, 2015, 2016).

in this current time and dealing with the issues that we are dealing with today' (E-Quill Media 2017a). Where the difference between the fictional Charlie Chan and Sonny Liew is clear, Chin's Troy character and his public persona are virtually indistinguishable. He claims, 'I don't repackage myself in shrink wrap to try to pass off as new' (Koe 2012).

Thus, while Liew presents Charlie as close to the traditional model of the artist, who separates himself from entrepreneurial activity through agents or by withdrawing from the market, Chin's Troy fully inhabits the tensions of the contemporary creative worker, who, as Laikwan Pang puts it, 'simultaneously embodies two seemingly oppositional logics … [the creative worker] must both self-actualise and fulfill competitive market demands at the same time' (Pang 2012: 51–52).[5] Chin provides detailed depictions of his work life – long days working alone in his room; meetings with agents in Singapore and Taiwan, the frustrations of working with clients who continually change their demands, weighing the pros and cons of taking government funding, displaying his comics and meeting with fans at festivals, teaching and lecturing. We see that, as a creative worker, his work life and personal life are inseparable. As he catches up with his friends from school, the army, and New York, they wonder about how they are going to be portrayed in his comics.

Chin's critique of neoliberal development is subtle. He is especially interested in institutions – school, the army, the music industry and democracy. He examines each of these institutions primarily through their effects on the emotional life of ordinary citizens. The first time I encountered *The Resident Tourist* was in a short piece in the first *Liquid City* collection, 'Otah Tree'. In it, Troy and his friend Mint, another returnee from New York, go to visit a favourite childhood spot of Mint's, only to discover that it is now a construction site, soon to be a car park. They squat there and eat the nostalgic snack they have bought anyway. As they get ready to leave, Mint asks, 'If I hadn't come here, I'd still believe that my tree's standing alive. Would that have been better or worse?' Troy's voice-over captions say,

> In the six months since my return to Singapore, I've only visited a very small handful of my old haunts. I don't go out because I have too much work to draw. No, that's not it. I don't because … I can't answer that question.

This vignette is typical of many in *The Resident Tourist* series. It presents a banal experience with which readers in any Asian city (and many other parts of the world as well) can identify. Chin attempts to peel back layers of rationalisation common in everyday discourse to reach a more complex emotional contradiction. He reserves judgment, but points to the contradictions raised by contemporary social conditions – here, raising the question of whether a sense of social/national belonging is possible when physical traces of memory are erased, while also questioning the value of nostalgia.

Chin pays careful attention to the emotional effects of development and its institutions not only on young people like himself, who are already part of the new economy, but on those who believe in the older ideology of the PAP, and find themselves somehow falling behind. Chin records several instances in which the bare facts of his own life – his abandonment of a stable job in the US for creative, freelance work at home – arouse sudden and

[5] Pang sees this tension as intensifying with the development of the creative industries discourse. It should be noted that the image of the Bohemian artist struggling alone to be free from the pressures of the market is the product of a few trends within the history of Western art and literature, and that this tension, as well as the gig economy, has characterised the career of many artists at least since the nineteenth century; the career of Charles Dickens, for example, is closer to this model than to that of the Romantic poet or Impressionist painter.

excessive anger in strangers, men both old and young, who identify with the values of the older Singapore dream, of working hard, making money, providing for family.

A key character here is Kampong Boy, Troy's grade school friend. Kampong Boy is an ambivalent figure. In many ways, he represents the mainstream from which Troy is completely alienated. He has abandoned social work, the career for which he was trained, because it doesn't make enough money, and he is constantly trying the get-rich schemes of assorted business gurus. He even thinks about writing his own comics once he sees that Troy has started to make some money from it.

The Resident Tourist is psychologically realist in its character construction, with each of the main characters having clearly defined personalities. Nonetheless, it is possible to read the relationship between Kampong Boy and Troy as allegorical. The *kampong*, or village, is a major figure of nostalgia within Singaporean discourse, used by both the promoters of development and those critical of it, and Kampong Boy seems to be the one who most clearly represents a dominant Singaporean self-image. He is similar, in some ways, to the characters in the extremely popular Singaporean comedy film, *I Not Stupid* (Neo 2002), who are 'stock figures and stereotype images, [but] also endearingly familiar' (Yao 2007: 142). Like several of the characters in *I Not Stupid*, Kampong Boy exhibits 'the uncertain feeling that is a mixture of jealousy, competitiveness, and self-interest' (2007: 148) which Singaporeans call *kiasu*. Kiasu means 'fear of losing out' in Hokkien, and one of the most successful Singaporean cartoon characters of all time, Mr. Kiasu, became an ambivalent national stereotype in the 1990s. In Yao Souchou's analysis, the film both resonates with the undercurrent of Singaporeans' dissatisfaction with their government and society, but also undercuts its own critique, because 'the State would almost certainly agree with some of the film's messages: that parents should not pressure their children in rote learning, and that independent thinking should be valued over blind submissiveness' (152).

The comfortable complicity that Yao finds between the humorous kiasu stereotype and the PAP's turn to the project of socially engineering creativity is undercut in Kampong Boy, but not because *The Resident Tourist* advocates regime change. Rather, it is the emotional realism of the narrative that forces the reader to critique the idea that engineering creativity will be easy and unambiguously a good thing. Kampong Boy is a figure of pathos as well as humour, a 'loser' unable to fit into the new economy or the middle class society of his generation, despite his extreme identification with the mainstream. Part of Troy's ambivalence about Singapore is related to his guilt over having betrayed Kampong Boy when they were school children, even though in Part 6 the adult Troy cuts him out of his life once again.

Although Chin is very critical of the pressure put on Singaporean children to get good grades, get a good job and earn money, the contrast between Kampong Boy and Troy is presented not as a simple contrast between old 'Asian values' of rote learning and sheer diligence, and new 'creative values' fostered by a less regimented education system. Rather, the two characters can be seen as embodying maladaptive vs. adaptive ways of bridging the gap between old and new Singapores. Troy represents a model of the creative worker that is different from both the classical Western individual genius model and the model presented by Charlie of the politically motivated artist whose innovation lies in appropriation and adaptation.

Unlike the vast majority of comics artists, including Liew, who profess a childhood love of drawing and have formal training in fine art or graphic design, Chin is unique in that he claims to have been very bad at and even to have hated art as a child. He began drawing only because his psychiatrist asked him to as part of his therapy. He taught himself to draw (via online courses and lots of practice) mid-life, only because he wanted to continue to tell his stories through comics, and the reader can see the gradual refinement of his skills over the course of the series. Ironically, the qualities that make him a successful cartoonist are actually the same ones that made him a successful financial officer – not just hard work, but an orientation toward acquiring skill that one might characterise as obsessive-compulsive. Troy's obsessiveness is a focus of his psychotherapy, something he and his psychiatrist see as a source of great suffering, but also adaptability and success. In other words, Chin implicitly proposes that OCD could be seen as a national resource, a way of thinking about the value of the risk-seeking orientation the PAP now seeks to encourage that recognises its ambivalence.

Aside from his obsessive-compulsive approach to craft, the other (equally ironic) source of Chin's creativity is his alienation from Singapore. In an interview, Chin says that one problem his therapist posed to him, and that *The Resident Tourist* continues to work through, is 'Why did I want to get out of Singapore in the first place? (E-Quill Media 2017b). It is his sense of simultaneously belonging and not belonging in both Singapore and New York, and his need to understand the relationship between mobility and creativity, that gives Chin what Audrey Yue (this volume) calls the 'diaspora advantage'.

One way that Chin's diaspora advantage plays out is in his ability to construct the sense of a public or a community of similarly out-of-place people through visual and textual address. What the character quoted above who describes *The Resident Tourist* as using 'the visual style of manga' refers to is that Chin's drawing creates what Scott McCloud calls the 'masking effect'. The masking effect 'combines very iconic characters with unusually realistic backgrounds' which 'allows readers to mask themselves in a character and safely enter a sensually stimulating world' (McCloud 1993: 42–43). In *The Resident Tourist*, as in many Japanese manga, the human faces are relatively blank, lacking angles and texture, while the architectural backgrounds are almost photographically detailed. Chin is also a fan of video games, and he creates a similar sense of immersion to that experienced while gaming. He moves his characters through a wide range of environments – here, everyday Singapore sites from hawker centres to bedrooms to nature trails – and occasionally provides neighbourhood maps.

McCloud also argues that the gutter, the space between frames and pages, is another kind of invitation to projection, requiring the reader to fill in gaps in the story, and thus enter into an imaginative co-narration with the artist. Chin is a master of the gutter. For example, the reader is drawn into Chin's artistic process in Figure 3. The two-page depiction of Troy's daily work begins with an image of birds flying under clouds, and then moves to a blank piece of paper and instruments on Troy's desk. The relationship between these two images is left to the reader – we might interpret the birds, a traditional symbol of freedom, as an inspirational view that Troy is seeing from his window, or read the gap between the open sky and the desk as a kind of cinematic microscoping, reflecting the psychic enclosure and pressure of the space/time of creative work. Through his use of mysterious spaces between events and chronotopes, Chin also makes the reader complicit in a co-construction of a mundane, emotional history of Singapore's development that is starkly contrasted with the official history that pervades the discourses of institutions.

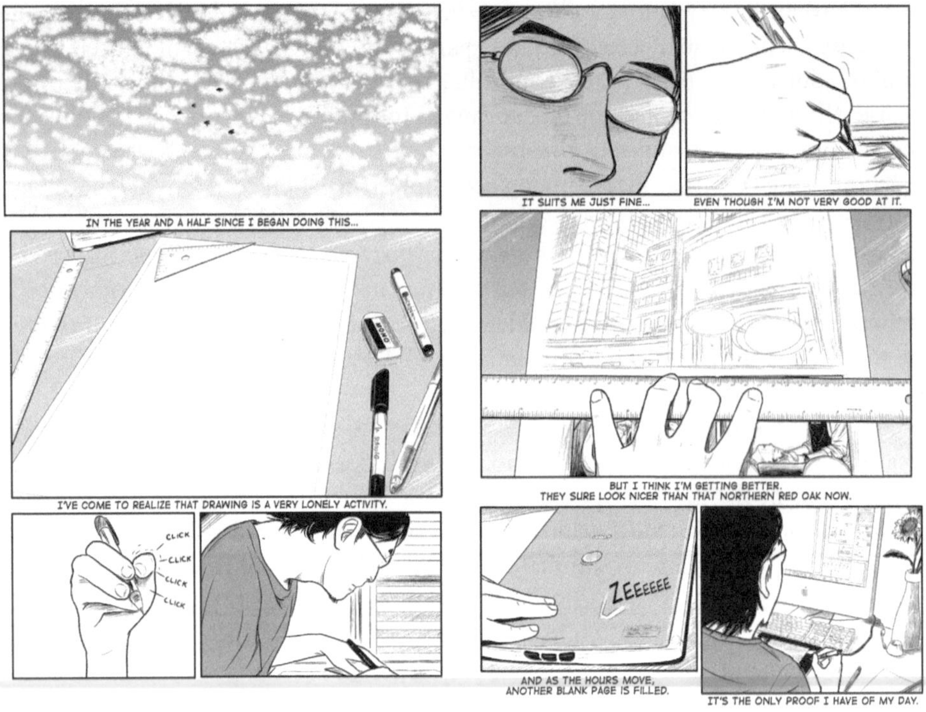

Figure 3. Chin's use of the gutter, and the refusal of complete emotional transparency, to draw the reader into complicity with his embodied, obsessive artistic process. (Reproduced with permission of Troy Chin.)

The invitation to the reader to participate in this unofficial historical vision is underlined by other techniques as well. For instance, Chin draws himself as the only character whose eyes are never visible – we only see the blank lenses of his glasses. Thus, although *The Resident Tourist* is an autobiography that is very explicit about its author's personality and point of view, there is always a way in which complete, fixed understanding of his thoughts and emotions is refused; readers can only imagine themselves into Troy's situation, while constantly reminded that however they feel they identify with him, they are projecting, filling in a blank

Complicity is thematised in Chin's mode of direct address as well. Chin is clearly addressing an international audience – he often gives definitions of Singaporean slang terms, even including a glossary at the end of Part 6, and the narratorial voice-overs sometimes begin with phrases like, 'for those of you who didn't grow up in Singapore … ' But at the same time, he is also clearly writing for other Singaporeans, for instance in a scene where the caption text describes one of adolescent Troy's neighbours:

> I can understand why some Singaporeans are put off by the way I speak and act today. I had the same reaction when I met the guy above, who was presumably local, but behaved like he was from somewhere else. You know exactly what I'm talking about.

At times, Chin, like Liew, adopts a sort of visual Verfremdungseffekt, breaking the frame to directly challenge the reader to adopt an active and critical stance toward taken-for-granted discourses of Singaporean history and identity (Figures 4 and 5).

Figure 4. Frontispiece from *The Art of Charlie Chan Hock Chye*. (Reproduced with permission of Sonny Liew and Epigram Books Pte Ltd.)

Figure 5. Direct address in *The Resident Tourist.* (Reproduced with permission of Troy Chin.)

While Liew's pastiche of styles and different tellings of the Singapore Story encourage a sort of Brechtian stance in the reader, a stepping outside of all of the juxtaposed positions into an intellectually critical position, Chin's use of blankness and narrative gaps encourages not merely emotional identification but active complicity. Where Charlie is an unreliable narrator, focused on the creation of possible pasts and futures through fantasy, Troy is an incomplete narrator. His realism is aimed not so much at eliciting identification with Troy as a character as at eliciting identification with the shared social reality he describes, and a consciousness of how the reader participates in it.

Conclusion

Sonny Liew's and Troy Chin's graphic novels challenge the ideology of illiberal pragmatism, not just through critiquing specific policies but through questioning the meaning of pragmatism itself. The PAP has resolved the tension between their desire to develop creative industries and their desire to maintain control over the behaviour and worldview of the population partly through direct measures such as censorship and education programmes. But more relevantly here, it has tried to absorb the arts into the discourse of pragmatism, by defining art's function as contributing to national economic growth, not only as a form of commodity in itself but as an attraction for tourists, foreign investors and the local middle class. Sonny Liew and Troy Chin are both engaged in the project of developing Singaporean creativity but they draw on an alternative tradition in the arts in which the function of art is not simply to be decorative, or emotionally moving but to provoke critical thinking, especially critical thinking about how society is organised. For both artists, the problem of developing creative capacities and the problem of reconstructing Singaporean culture and identity are inseparable.

Reading *The Art of Charlie Chan* and *The Resident Tourist* together, we get a sense of how the relationship between self-identity and the creative economy have become increasingly intertwined over the past 20 years. In the 1960s, when Charlie's partner leaves to get married and find a more lucrative job so that he can raise a family, they both see this as a personal sacrifice, as giving up on making more meaningful contributions to the nation. In post-financial crisis Singapore, Troy Chin's opposite choice, to leave a lucrative career to make comics, leaves him open to constant accusations of being 'un-Singaporean', of betraying the nation.

Both Liew and Chin seek to model new creative and national identities, using very different strategies. The questions facing Singapore's developing creative industries are very different from those that have been posed in the United States. Scholars in the US have generally started from an assumption of a separation of artists from capitalism, and focused on how to merge the two – of how to make entrepreneurs out of artists, or how to infuse creativity into business models (Florida 2002; Ross 2003; Win 2014). These two Singaporean artists see the problem as one of the transformation of social and psychic structures, and are more concerned with questions of how to rethink the relationship between creativity and identity. Sonny Liew and Troy Chin each model new ways to manage the contradictions between the value of pragmatism, as it has long been defined by the PAP, and the critical consciousness and ability to imagine alternative futures that they see as crucial to meeting the challenges of a small and marginal nation within a global economy increasingly based on creative production.

Acknowledgements

I want to thank Sonny Liew and Troy Chin for their generosity in allowing me to reproduce their artwork, and Sonny Liew and Edmund Wee for accepting my interviews. I also thank the participants in the Inter-Asia Cultural Studies conference in Surabaya in 2015 and the Labor of Animation conference at the Institute of Ethnology, Academia Sinica, in 2016 who gave me excellent feedback on presentations from which this paper developed (especially Amie Parry, Audrey Yue, Chua Beng-huat, Naifei Ding, Chien-ting Lin, and Paul Manning), as well as the anonymous reviewers for this issue of *Culture, Theory and Critique.*

Disclosure statement

No potential conflict of interest was reported by the author.

Funding

Research for this paper was funded in part by two grants from the Ministry of Science and Technology, Taiwan (MOST 103-2410-H-001-056 and MOST 105-2410-H-001-082-MY3).

References

Bahng, Aimee. 2015. 'The Cruel Optimism of Asian Futurity and the Reparative Practices of Sonny Liew's *Malinky Robot*'. In David Roh, Betsy Huang, and Greta Niu (eds), *Techno-Orientalism: Imagining Asia in Speculative Fiction, History, and Media.* Rutgers University Press, 163–179.

Chin, Troy. 2008. 'The Resident Tourist: Otah Tree'. In Sonny Liew (ed), *Liquid City* Volume One. Berkeley, CA: Image Comics, 28–37.

Chin, Troy. 2009. *The Resident Tourist* Part 3. (originally appeared August 2008 on www.drearyweary.com). Singapore: Dreary Weary Comics.

Chin, Troy. 2010. *The Resident Tourist* Part 4. Singapore: Dreary Weary Comics.

Chin, Troy. 2011a. *The Resident Tourist* Part 1. (originally appeared November 2007 on www.drearyweary.com). Singapore: Dreary Weary Comics.

Chin, Troy. 2011b. *The Resident Tourist* Part 2. (originally appeared February 2008 on www.drearyweary.com). Singapore: Dreary Weary Comics.

Chin, Troy. 2011c. *The Resident Tourist* Part 5. Singapore: Dreary Weary Comics.

Chin, Troy. 2014. *The Resident Tourist* Part 6. Singapore: Math Paper Press.

Chin, Troy. 2015. *The Resident Tourist* Part 7. Singapore: Math Paper Press.

Chin, Troy. 2016. *The Resident Tourist* Part 8. Singapore: Math Paper Press.

Chua, Beng-huat. 1995. *Communicative Ideology and Democracy in Singapore*. London: Routledge.

E-Quill Media. 2017a. Troy Chin on Writing Comic Books in Singapore. *E-Quill Media*. Available online at https://www.youtube.com/watch?v=e6m6G_1rV54

E-Quill Media. 2017b. The Pain and Suffering of Comics Artist Troy Chin. *E-Quill Media*. Available online at https://www.youtube.com/watch?v=P7Cr7UH48VA

Florida, Richard. 2002. *The Rise of the Creative Class, and How It's Transforming Work, Leisure, Community, and Everyday Life*. New York: Basic Books.

Guimares, Graca. n.d. 'Sonny Liew Interview'. *Banana Writers*. Available online at www.bananawriters.com/sonnyliewinterview

Han, Kirsten. 2015. 'The Singapore Government Pulled the Funding for This Comic Book, and Now Readers Only Want It More'. *GlobalVoices*. https://globalvoices.org/2015/06/04/the-singapore-government-pulled-the-funding-for-this-comic-book-and-now-readers-only-want-it-more/

Koe, Amanda Lee. 2012. 'A Social Experiment with Troy Chin'. www.poskod.sg/Posts/2012/10/18/A-Social-Experiment-with-Troy-Chin.

Kong, Lily, Gibson, Chris, Khoo, Louisa-May, and Semple, Anne-Louise. 2006. 'Knowledges of the Creative Economy: Towards a Relational Geography of Diffusion and Adaptation in Asia'. *Asia Pacific Viewpoint* 47:2, 173–194.

Lent, John. 2015. *Asian Comics*. Jackson, MS: University of Mississippi Press.

Liew, Sonny. 2015. *The Art of Charlie Chan Hock Chye*. Singapore: Epigram Books.

Lim, Cheng Tju. 1997. 'Singapore Political Cartooning'. *Asian Journal of Social Science* 25:1, 125–150.

Lim, Cheng Tju. 2014. 'Current Trends in Singapore Comics: When Autobiography is Mainstream'. *Kyoto Review of Southeast Asia* 2: 16. Available online at http://kyotoreview.org/issue-16/current-trends-in-singapore-comics-when-autobiography-is-mainstream/attachment/singapore_comics-banner/.

McCloud, Scott. 1993. *Understanding Comics: The Invisible Art*. New York: HarperCollins.

Media Development Authority. 2002. *Creative Industries Development Strategy: Propelling Singapore's Creative Economy*. Singapore: Ministry of Information, Communication and the Arts.

Neo, Jack. 2002. *I Not Stupid*. Mediacorp Raintree Pictures, United International Pictures, Singapore.

Ong, Aihwa. 2006. *Neoliberalism as Exception: Mutations in Citizenship and Sovereignty*. Durham, NC: Duke University Press.

Pang, Laikwan. 2012. *Creativity and Its Discontents: China's Creative Industries and Intellectual Property Rights Offenses*. Durham, NC: Duke University Press.

Patten, Fred. 2007. 'Simba versus Kimba: The Pride of Lions'. In Alan Cholodenko (ed), *The Illusion of Life II: More Essays on Animation*. Sydney: Power Publications, 275–313.

Pinion, Kyle. 2016. 'Review: *The Art of Charlie Chan Hock Chye* is 2016s First Superlative Graphic Novel'. *Toucan: the official blog of Comic-Con and Wondercon*. Available online.

Ross, Andrew. 2003. *No-Collar: The Humane Workplace and Its Hidden Costs*. Philadelphia: Temple University Press.

Smith, Philip. 2016. 'Nation-building, Censorship, and "Ill-Will" in Singaporean Comics'. *The Journal of Popular Culture* 49:1, 97–115.

Warner, Michael. 2002. *Publics and Counterpublics*. New York: Zone Books.

Wee, C. J. Wan-ling. 2007. *The Asian Modern: Culture, Capitalist Development, Singapore*. Hong Kong: Hong Kong University Press.

Win, Thet Shein. 2014. 'Marketing the Entreprenuerial Artist in the Innovation Age: Aesthetic Labor, Artistic Subjectivity, and the Creative Industries'. *Anthropology of Work Review* XXXV:1, 2–13.

Yao, Souchou. 2007. *Singapore: The State and the Culture of Excess*. London: Routledge.

Yue, Audrey. 2012. 'Introduction: Queer Singapore: A Critical Introduction'. In Audrey Yue and Ju Zubillaga-Pow (eds), *Queer Singapore: Illiberal Citizenship and Mediated Cultures*. Hong Kong: Hong Kong University Press, 1–28.

6 The 'diaspora advantage' of Pauline Chan (1956–): from multicultural filmmaker to cultural broker

Audrey Yue

ABSTRACT
This is the first academic paper to critically introduce and document the 30-year screen career of Pauline Chan, Australia's highest profile Chinese film director, television actress and media producer. Sydney-based, Vietnam-born, Hong Kong-educated and US-trained, Chan has directed six films, starred in 14 and produced four television series and films. Despite her prolific career, there has been no sustained research on her profile and repertoire. This paper evaluates the evolution of Chan's career using the diaspora 'advantage' as a new approach. Characterised by mobility rather than culturalism, the term refers to the benefits brought by and skills of diaspora groups that have allowed them to flourish as transnational actors able to leverage resources in both their countries of origin and settlement. It begins by elaborating how Chan's diaspora advantage has allowed her to challenge welfare multiculturalism and extend aesthetic multiculturalism. It further documents her transition from a multicultural filmmaker to a cultural intermediary by leveraging her diasporic advantage across the film sectors in China and Australia, and opening up new industrial routes outside of the confines of policy. Using interdisciplinary methods to screen biography that include interviews with the filmmaker, film archival research, critical cultural policy studies, and studies in Asian Australian cinema and political economy, this paper argues that the new approach of the diaspora advantage turns the deficit associated with the diaspora into a dividend that has the potential to rethink the imaginary between Asia and Australia.

1. Introduction

Pauline Chan is a Sydney-based, Vietnam-born, Hong Kong-educated, US-trained, Australian film director, television actress and media producer. In the 1980s when Australia was beginning to embrace multiculturalism, Chan was one of the first Chinese actresses to appear on Australian television, starring in high profile mini-series such as *Bangkok Hilton* (1989). In the 1990s, when Asian Australian cinema debuted with its migrant stories such as *Floating Life* (Clara Law 1996), Chan was one of its leading New Wave directors, introducing films such as *Traps* (1994), one of the first films to be shot in Vietnam after the American War. Since the 2000s, with screen policies promoting

Australian co-production with Asia, Chan has become the 'go-to' producer for brokering film partnerships with China. *33 Postcards*, her 2011 co-produced feature film with China, broke box office records for Australia, and introduced new funding and audience development strategies. To date, she has directed six films, starred in 14 and produced four television series and films. Despite her prolific career, a career that bends with, shapes and reflects key national and international directions in film and cultural policies, there has been no sustained research on her profile and repertoire.

This is the first academic paper to critically introduce and document the 30-year screen career of Chan. It formulates the 'diaspora advantage' as a new approach to consider her roles across television and film. The term refers to the benefits brought by and skills of diaspora groups that have allowed them to flourish as transnational actors able to leverage resources in both their countries of origin and settlement. The term highlights mobility rather than culturalism as a key factor for the advantage. This paper evaluates the evolution of Chan's roles against changing developments in multicultural and creative economic policies to show how, while Chan's career has blossomed under the auspices of these policies, it is her diasporic advantage that has enabled her to challenge policy's hegemony and create new aesthetic styles and industrial forms. It documents Chan's career in two phases. The first, in the 1980s and 1990s, is mapped against multicultural and creative national policy developments. While Chan 'arrived' on the scene following the access brought forth by welfare multiculturalism, it is the mobility of her diaspora advantage that has allowed her to leverage and extend aesthetic multiculturalism by 'worlding' Asia in Australia. Rather than tell stories about Asians in Australia, her diaspora advantage has enabled her to pluralise Asia and create a new polycentrism to problematise the role of Australia in Asia. Further evaluating the second and current phase of Chan's career from the late 2000s, a period that coincided with the development of screen convergence and film co-production policies that saw new modes of filmmaking in Australia and across the world, this paper shows how Chan continues to leverage her diasporic advantage by becoming a cultural intermediary, in particular, brokering across the film sectors in China and Australia, and opening up new industrial routes outside of the confines of policy. Critically documenting Chan's career using interdisciplinary methods to screen biography that include interviews with the filmmaker, film archival research, critical cultural policy studies, and studies in Asian Australian cinema and political economy, this paper argues that the new approach of the diaspora advantage turns the deficit associated with the diaspora into a dividend that has the potential to rethink the imaginary between Asia and Australia.

2. The diaspora advantage

The concept of the diaspora describes groups dispersed from their original homelands. Classical typologies include the Greeks, Jews and Armenians who escaped religious persecution, and the overseas Chinese and Indians who departed as indentured labourers and economic migrants. Diaspora studies arose in the mid-1990s to further conceptualise the mobility and sociology of these groups, in particular highlighting the differences between first and second generation diasporas: the former experience deep homeland nostalgia and create imagined hostland communities while the latter embody contrapuntal belonging and are at home in both homeland and hostland cultures (Hall 1990; Quayson 2013).

Drawing on the duality of their identities and connections, one of the key characteristics of diasporic groups is the formation of triangular trans-state relationships with old homelands and new countries of settlement. Common here are economic networks of transnational entrepreneurship comprising new business organisations built by individuals and groups in currently adopted countries while drawing on resources from their countries of origin (Liu 2012; Honig et al. 2010). The 'diaspora advantage' refers to how their use of language skills, cultural understandings and global networks are deployed as opportunities for the transnational circulation of ideas, people, capital and commerce (Rizvi et al 2016: vi). In home countries, these benefits are most notable in how overseas remittances have transformed primary family support, led to the rise of peripheral urban centres and become a key contributor to national economies (McGregor 2014; Semyonov and Gorodzeisky 2008). Across bilateral business networks, migrants' role in the exchange of information has also significantly increased global trade (Sangita 2013). Diasporic entrepreneurialism has the potential to boost the international engagement of host countries, especially across the creative industries with their culture-led appeals for soft power.

While diaspora advantage is a recently coined term, it draws on an established interdisciplinary field that examines the cause and effect of such an advantage. In diasporic and transnational Chinese cultural studies, for example, earlier revisionist studies focusing on the flexibility of heritage (such as Confucianism or *guanxi*) (Wang 1993) have been displaced by studies on Chineseness as a transnational force delinked from the nation-state or entwined with the economic rise of the Asia-Pacific region, in particular China (Ong and Nonini 1997; Liu 2012). More recent studies, however, have begun to theorise diasporic Chinese entrepreneurialism as a consequence of migration rather than culturalism. Examining the global history of overseas Chinese businesses, McKeown (2000) unravels how historical and structural practices such as weak protection of legal contracts and official encouragement of merchant self-regulation were instrumental in the formation of diasporic business networks that flourished with mobility and trade. These practices continue to resonate in the present through the attributes of smart engagement exhibited by diasporic cultural practitioners.

Arts, media and culture have become key sectors where diasporic practitioners have independently forged transnational engagement that have oftentimes gone unrecognised by state organisations. Evident through partnerships in international art exhibitions, film festivals, and media collaborations, these culture workers are quick to embrace emergent opportunities, take more risk, and are less reliant on government support and funding. They bring skills and assets including 'peer-to-peer trust, self-reliance, a focus on impact, a high degree of literacy in digital and traditional media, autonomous organisations, and a commitment to building long-term relationships' (Holden 2013: 3; Quoted in Ang et al. 2015: 137). They also possess deep understanding of local contexts and sensitivities, are eager to acquire requisite networks, rely on private funding, and need little encouragement to engage internationally (Fitzgerald and Chau 2014; Quoted in Ang et al. 2015: 137).

Significant here is how these skills are accumulated to self-optimise chances of adaptation in migrants' countries of settlement. Instead of relying solely on the diversity domains of race or ethnicity, what distinguishes this group is their diversity of human, social and motivational capitals. Human capital refers to the skills and experience already acquired in home countries; social capital refers to the relationships and network of connections from countries of origin or birth; motivational capital refers to how motivations such as the economic push–pull theory of migration (Borjas 1989), as well as ability to integrate and adapt, impact upon the management of careers in destination countries. To accommodate local labour markets, workers deploy and accrue these capitals to strategically expand their value. These capitals inform the diversity of career capital and play an important role in the source of competitive advantage (Zikic 2015). Important to note is that while these capitals are embodied and agential, they are also embedded in unequal power structures that shape the racialised, classed and gendered diasporic subject. What counts as 'advantage' is accorded differential cultural values, such as those that separate skilled migrants from guest workers.

Significant here too is the way in which the diaspora advantage is mobilised. Rather than define these skills as sociological and substantive traits of groupism, it is more productive to consider diaspora 'as a category of practice' (Brubaker 2005: 12). As practice, the diaspora advantage is less a descriptive term and more an analytical lens for evaluating the alliances that are produced between countries of origin and settlement. These alliances take place across different scales, through various forms of interdependencies between actors, communities and states, and transcend categories such as local/global and home/host. Recent studies have described such a practice of cooperation through the concept of assemblage:

> [They] are the product of multiple determinations and not reducible to a single logic: 'They do not always involve new forms, but forms that are shifting, in formation, or at stake. As a composite concept, the term "global assemblage" thus points to inherent tensions: global implies broadly encompassing, seamless, and mobile; assemblage implies heterogeneous, contingent, unstable, partial, and situated.' (Collier and Ong 2005: 12; Quoted in Carment and Sadjed 2017: 261–262)

The diaspora advantage creates new transnational partnerships through the formation of such an assemblage. These partnerships are not only transactional; they are also transgressive in their exchange through the productive and permanent transformations they bring.

In sum, rather than bridge nation-states, the diaspora advantage has enabled workers to deploy career capital diversity, assemble new cultures of cooperation and become independent actors. The following shows how the benefits of migration and mobility, rather than culturalism, have enabled Chan to navigate changing screen policy regimes in Australia to create new aesthetic styles and industrial forms that have challenged hegemonic norms.

3. From welfare to aesthetic multiculturalism: worlding Asia in Australia

Chan was born in Vietnam in 1956. Her Chinese mother fled Hong Kong to escape the Japanese occupation during the Second World War. Her father was a Vietnamese businessman who was imprisoned for his capitalist activities when Vietnam became a communist country. When the Vietnam war broke out, she and her brother were sent to Hong Kong to study. Chan migrated to Australia in 1980 after completing her high school in Hong Kong and university training in the United States. Even before arriving in Australia, she was already exposed to the workings of various film industries, having grown up with parents and grandparents active in the entertainment scene in China in the 1930s and

1940s; trained in ULCA's media school; and starred in minor roles as film extras in the Hong Kong martial arts film industry during the 1970s. Chan's screen career in Australia began and flourished between the 1980s and 1990s. During this period, she starred in 16 television series and directed two feature films and three short films. This period saw the ascendency of multiculturalism and the emergence of a national creative cultural policy. While Chan was a beneficiary of these policies, her aesthetic style incorporated career capital diversity and allowed her to challenge the welfare agenda of multiculturalism.

Introduced in 1973 with the demise of the White Australia policy, multiculturalism was instituted as a policy and ideology for social cohesion. It emerged as a set of integration programmes that catered to the welfare needs of migrants from non-English speaking backgrounds, and by the 1980s, was elevated to a national policy that aimed to enrich the cultural diversity of everyday life (Jupp 1996).[1] Multiculturalism arose and flourished not without contestations. The Right has criticised its privileging of minority rights that entrenched division (Viviani 1999) while the Left viewed it as a form of boutique multiculturalism (Fish 1997) that maintained the hegemony of white monoculturalism (Hage 1998). Despite these contestations, by the 1990s multiculturalism was adopted across the arts sectors to address equity in representation and provide access for ethnic minority culture workers (Gunew and Rizvi 1994).

Four key developments characterised the arts and media culture of this period. Australia introduced its first cultural policy agenda, Creative Nation, in 1994, that encouraged creative innovation through multicultural diversity and indigeneity (DCA 1994). With this move and in the same year, the nation's multicultural broadcaster Special Broadcasting Service (SBS) established its film commissioning arm Special Broadcasting Service Independent (SBSi) which produced 810 multicultural-themed film titles during its active years between 1994 and 2007. Following these initiatives, the term 'multicultural cinema' (O'Regan 1996) was coined to collectively group together a body of films that celebrated stories about diverse representations of migrants, and to recognise the positive contributions of non-English speaking communities. In the film sector, this period saw the arrival of the Asian Australian New Wave (Khoo, Smaill and Yue 2013), a group led by Chan and which also included the Macau-born Tony Ayers and Malaysian-born Teck Tan. They benefitted from the diversity access of the film school, and graduated at a time that coincided with the 'coming of age' of an Asian community that was becoming visible in the public sphere. These policies and programmes led to the rise of welfare and aesthetic multiculturalism, two forms of cultural value that underpin the evaluation of multicultural arts and media (Yue and Khan 2014).

In Australia's cultural policy development, multiculturalism has two definitions: a narrow definition that explicitly addresses migrant disadvantage, the problem of minority access and the need to celebrate ethnic difference and serve cultural maintenance; and a wider definition that implicitly addresses the broader domain of cultural diversity, including multiple identities and hybridities, and a global cosmopolitan post-national mainstream (Cope et al 2003: 11). These definitions place multicultural arts and media in a continuum, from the intrinsic value of aesthetics to the instrumental value for social

[1] As indigenous and multicultural histories have developed as separate white/Aboriginal and white/multicultural (including Asians and Europeans) discourses due to their distinct structures of bureaucratic control, indigenous Australians are positioned outside of multicultural policy and discourse.

inclusion, and highlight the tension between aesthetic and welfare multiculturalism. Such a tension arose from the politics of arts funding. National arts and screen funding agencies, such as the Australian Council or Screen Australia, have traditionally fostered work deemed to be of 'excellence' and measured against a particular (usually Eurocentric) aesthetic standard. This has tended to perpetuate hierarchies of taste, privileging 'high' art forms at the expense of more 'grassroots', 'community'-based or culturally diverse forms of artistic expression. Commentators were concerned whether existing funding policies and frameworks of aesthetic evaluation were inclusive of migrant communities and artists, and whether these groups had the same sorts of access to resources and opportunities as 'mainstream' communities (Hawkins 1993). To address elitist funding, another criterion based on 'access' was introduced to democratise the arts. It is this principle of 'access' that has traditionally defined the parameters of what is known in Australia as 'multicultural arts'. However, this resulted in a historical association between 'ethnic' or 'multicultural arts' with 'community'-based or 'amateur' artistic expression, an association that is part of a broader discourse of 'welfare' multiculturalism. It is in response to this association that there has been a more recent shift towards 'aesthetic' multiculturalism. Aesthetic multiculturalism draws on the broader definition of multicultural arts identified above, is viewed as 'cosmopolitan' in its orientation, and is usually associated with the work of professional rather than amateur artists. Within and against these contexts, Chan benefitted from the welfare agenda of multiculturalism but actively applied her career capital diversity to extend aesthetic multiculturalism.

After migrating to Australia and working for a few years, Chan enrolled in the Australian Film Television and Radio School (AFTRS) in 1986. The high costs associated with film school training led her to extend her studies across five years. To support film school, she sought work in the sector. This stint honed her filmmaking skills and extended her networks. Already at this early stage in her new country, Chan sought to adapt to the local labour market by deploying her foreign and newly acquired skills. Her diaspora advantage is evident in the way she built upon motivational, human and social capitals. Keen to be a part of her new country of residence in general and the Australian film sector in particular, her desire to enter the local industry is guided by motivational capital. This is related to her desire to not only translate her foreign knowledge but also accumulate local human capital to add to the skills and experience brought from Hong Kong and the US. These factors to adapt and integrate are also evident in her determination to build new social relationships and connections. It was during this period that she began her collaborations with George Miller, an Australian director best known for the *Mad Max* (1979–2015) and *Happy Feet* (2006–2011) franchises. Chan found work at the production house, Kennedy Miller (now known as Kennedy Miller Mitchell), co-founded by Miller. Kennedy Miller was one of the most innovative, established and successful production houses in Australia, especially during the golden years in the 1980s when it pioneered the mini television series and made-for-television films. These novel forms raised the quality of television and ushered in the beginnings of film and television convergence. This practice, now common in the industry, refers to the range of production and distribution synergies across the film and television sectors such as the distribution of cinema by television or the made-for-television film streamed on-demand that have arisen as a result of the digital post-broadcast mediascape. Two new production finance structures also encouraged Kennedy Miller's growth: the 10BA tax incentive scheme that allowed companies to claim tax deductions for donations to the sector, and the Commercial Television Production Fund, an annual AUD$20 million a year programme of the Creative Nation national cultural policy (Turnbull and Collins 2001). Chan worked on many of Kennedy Miller's quality television productions in a variety of roles: film research for in-house directors such as Philip Noyce, Chris Noonan and John Duigan; production assistant; runner; and film script translator (Yue 2016). She also acted in two of their high-profile series: the ten-part series *Vietnam* (dirs. Duigan and Noonan 1987) and the three-part *Bangkok Hilton* (dir. Cameron, 1989) that both starred a young Nicole Kidman.

As an actress, Chan's television work is minor despite being cast in 16 series and telemovies. She acted in below the line roles and was always stereotyped as an Asian woman (Chinese or Vietnamese or Thai), playing someone's kindly aunt (e.g., *Winners*, dirs. Bennett and Cox 1985) or just an unimportant bystander (e.g., *Breathing Under Water*, dir. Dermody 1992), and as victims of war (e.g., *Sword of Honour*, dirs. Amenta and Millar 1986; *Paradise Road*, dir. Beresford 1997), organised crime (e.g., *The Saint: Fear in the Fun Park*, dir. Crombie 1989; *Cassidy*, dir. Schultz 1989), troubled youth (e.g., *The Sugar Factory*, dir. Carter 1998) and corrupt government (e.g., *Grass Roots*, dir. Andrikidis 2000–2003). Even in a long-standing series like *G.P. (1989–1996*, Australian Broadcasting Corporation), a series about a general medical practice, which has eight seasons and 318 episodes, Chan only attained a minor role in one episode.

These stereotypes and their ideologies of casting conformed to the strategy of welfare multiculturalism that aimed to increase access (e.g., Chan gained entry in the predominantly white industry) without concomitantly positively lifting representations of minority people. Welfare multiculturalism reproduced a monocultural image of Australian society, as evident in the aforementioned titles of productions set in Australia. It also perpetuated the white Australian imaginary of Asia as a cultural threat that has to be contained, evident, for example, in two successful and popular series set in Asia. In *Vietnam* and *Bangkok Hilton*, where Chan respectively plays a village peasant (Lien) who falls in love with an Australian soldier and becomes a revolutionary fighter, and a sympathetic warden (Pretty Warden), Vietnam is constructed as a war jungle that has to be tamed by heroic white soldiers and Thailand is constructed through the horror of the wrongful incarceration of innocent white women. These gendered representations repeat the Orientalist stereotype of Asia as primitive and backward, and reflect an industry notorious for its dominant Anglo-Saxon European casting. This prejudice persists, evident in a recent national screen report showing non-European actors making up seven per cent of the lead roles compared to 17 per cent of the general population (Screen Australia 2016). Here, stereotyping presents a big obstacle to the diaspora advantage. By consigning otherness to ethnicity, stereotyping elides the work-related core competencies skilled migrants can bring. Against these constraints, it is not surprising that despite being the lead Vietnamese actor in *Vietnam*, Chan's other roles in the series – as script researcher, director assistant and technical advisor – were not even credited.

By the time Chan graduated from film school in 1991, she was already quite well-known in the sector due to her association with Kennedy-Miller. Her three short films (*The Space between the Door* [1990], *Hang Up* [1990] and *Dusty Hearts* [1991]), films made when she was at film school, achieved numerous nominations and won multiple international awards including a Special Mention Prize at the Torino International Festival of Young Cinema. It is in her role as director that she has challenged the stereotyping of welfare multiculturalism.

Chan overturned the ethnic filmmaker's burden of representation by creating new aesthetic and auteur styles for the mainstream filmmaking and film-going communities. Her aforementioned short films use Anglo Australian actors, deal with themes of love, romance and loss, and follow the conventions of art-house and noir. Experimental and avant-garde, and shot in black and white, they eschew any reference to 'ethnic filmmaking', refusing to tell stories about migrancy or Chinese marginality. Against these, it is no wonder that she was hailed as a 'Premier Australian filmmaker' by *Asia Week* magazine, and 'one of the most convincing successes of the new wave Australian filmmakers' by the French *Cahiers du Cinema* (quoted in ICFF 2016). On the heels of these successes, she quickly received funding to make her first feature film, *Traps* (1994).

Traps is set in Vietnam in the 1950s and tells the story of an English and Australian journalist-photographer couple who was sent there to cover a story about a French-owned plantation. The couple arrive as guests at the plantation and spend their time at a beautiful and decaying villa owned by the plantation foreman. They hope to rekindle their marriage in the exotic Far East but quickly become embroiled in the emotional, sexual and political tensions of their host and his beautiful daughter. Through the conflict between the host, his adopted country and his daughter, the film captures the last days of French-occupied Indochina.

As in Chan's short films, *Traps* casts non-Asians as key protagonists. The turmoil of a country struggling for independence is evoked through personal upheavals and the unravelling of deceit, illicit sex and betrayal. Chan adapted the story from an Australian novel *Dreamhouse* by Grenville (1986), and changed the original location of Tuscany to Vietnam. The shift of location is significant for Chan who wanted to return to Vietnam and seized this opportunity just when Vietnam was opening up to the world with the reform of *doi moi*,[2] and Australia was also opening up to Asia, as echoed by the then Prime Minister Paul Keating who boldly declared in 1992 that Australia was a part of Asia. Chan's own sense of displacement is mirrored through the struggle of the host's daughter, who was also the same age as the filmmaker when she left Vietnam. Chan's return migration situates Vietnam as the real protagonist of the film, as a yet-to-be nation torn apart by past colonial and future neo-colonial forces.

Traps costs AUD$3.5 m to make and only returned AUD$135,500 in sales. Its box office failure is reflected in dominant reviews of the film. In *Variety* magazine, renowned Australian film commentator David Stratton noted that although the film is 'very well-made', it 'lacks the dazzling style of the director's shorts' (Stratton 1994). In *New York Times*, Stephen Holden deplored the film's representation of sexual mores as 'naïve' and lamented its inability 'to develop credible characters or tell a complex story' (Holden 1995). In *LA Times*, Kevin Thomas also complained that the filmmaker 'lacks the skill and subtlety' to avoid the direct parallel between the personal and political (Thomas 1995). These reviews focus on the plot and ignore how the film can potentially provide a new way to engage with Asia.

[2]Initiated in 1986, '*doi moi*' refers to the opening up of Vietnam through economic rejuvenation and marks the country's transition from communism to socialist-oriented market economy.

With the demise of the White Australia policy and the inception of multiculturalism, Australian filmmakers had begun venturing to Asia to make films. Approximately 28 films were filmed in Asia between 1973 (the end of the White Australia policy) and 1994 (the release of *Traps*), and these fall broadly in three genres. The first is a small cluster of surfing films set in the Pacific and Indonesia about a group of surfers travelling from island to island in search of the perfect waves (e.g., *Kongs Island*, dir. McCoy 1980; *In Search of Tubular Swells*, dir. McCoy 1976; and *Storm Raiders*, dir. Hoole 1982). The second is a group of B-action films about corrupt governments or secret societies set in Hong Kong, Thailand or the Philippines (e.g., *That Lady from Peking*, dir. Davis 1975; *The Man from Hong Kong*, dir. Trenchard-Smith 1975; *Death Cheaters*, dir. Trenchard-Smith 1976; *Far East*, dir. Duigan 1982; *A Case of Honour*, dir. Romero 1989; *Sword of the Bushido*, dir. Carr 1989; and *Driving Force*, dir. Prowse 1989). The third is the war film about Australian soldiers in Asia, or crimes conducted by Japanese or Indonesia soldiers (e.g., *The Odd Angry Shot*, dir. Jeffrey 1979; *Attack Force Z*, dir. Burstall 1981; *The Year of Living Dangerously*, dir. Weir 1982; *Killer Instinct*, dir. Santiago 1987; *The Siege of Firebase Gloria*, dir. Trenchard-Smith 1989; and *Blood Oath*, dir. Wallace 1990) (see the Asian Australian Cinema database (2012)). These films follow the Orientalist motif of *Vietnam* and *Bangkok Hilton* discussed earlier which either represent Asia as an exotic paradise or a despotic dystopia. *Traps* presents a new imaginary of Asia, one that does not privilege Australia or repeat Australia's stereotype of Asia.

Told from the points of view of British, French, Australian and Vietnamese protagonists, and about the impacts of French and American colonisation in Vietnam, the film introduces a new practice to engage Asia from Australia. This practice can be likened to the concept of 'worlding', a term first coined by literary theorist Said (1983) and further developed by cultural scholars Wilson and Connery (2007). 'Worlding' offers three new ways of thinking about the world. First, as a critical category, worlding registers the presence of the text in the world by promoting multidisciplinary perspectives. Second, as a geographical category, worlding privileges other vantage points apart from the monocentrism of the West. Third, as a material category, worlding is grounded in social, political and historical specificities and attends to their contestations over territories, nationalities, ethnicities and identities. These categories of worlding allow the film to engage Asia from multiple sites other than Australia. First, it pluralises representations of Asia by showcasing polycentric perspectives from other Western countries such as Britain and France. Second, it privileges other vantage points such as that of the diasporic-returnee filmmaker or the settler colonial protagonist. Third, it grounds Vietnam within the contexts of its postcoloniality caught in the intersections of French-Indochinese decolonisation and Cold-War imperialism. In other words, rather than simply representing an Australian image of a fetishised or feared Asia, worlding multiplies the representations of Asia from other perspectives, including those from other Western centres. By portraying how the French, British and American also share similar benevolent presentations of Vietnam (as a disappearing colony, and as a colonial victim led astray by communism), the film calls to task Australia's complicity in the region, as a member of the Western colonial power bloc as well as its neocolonial Cold War artifice. The film's intermedial reference from its novel adaptation promises this potential by freeing the text from its Western-centric Italian setting and substituting it with Vietnam, and in the process, introducing a method to engage its new intertextuality through interculturalism. The film's genuine engagement with interculturalism is further supported in two ways. First, it departs from genre stereotyping by eschewing the penchants for war, surf or crime, in favour of an erotic thriller. While the erotic thriller genre has the tendency to objectify women (and Asian women in particular), Chan challenges this by (as stated earlier) not casting Asians as leads (hence, not reproducing the cliché of ethnicity or ethnic and diasporic filmmaking), and portraying her female protagonists as sexual agents (and in doing so, undoes the cliché of desexualisation that also plagues the myth of the stoic diasporic Asian woman). Second, it materialises its encounter by being one of the first films to be shot on location in Vietnam after the country begun its open-door reform. This is a rare feat for Western-based filmmakers at that time; even the awarded Vietnamese art house film *The Scent of the Green Papaya* (Tran 1993), released a year earlier and received the Camera d'Or at the 1993 Cannes Film Festival, was shot entirely in a studio in France. In the former, interculturalism is a filmmaking practice that allows the director to displace the specificity of ethnicity and tell generic women-centered stories about sex, desire and sexuality in such a way that promotes her and the female protagonists' agencies. In the latter, interculturalism is a mode of cross-cultural film production that has opened up the pathway for contemporary co-productions.

In sum, Chan's career capital diversity offers new potential to make films that challenge the ethnic burden of representation presented by Australia's Anglo-centered policy and aesthetic norms. She arrived on the film scene at a time when the country embraced multiculturalism that opened up access to film schools and introduced diversity representation on the screen. In her minor acting roles, she turned her diaspora disadvantage into a movement that informed the makings of a multicultural cinema. More significantly, it is through her roles as film research assistant, script researcher and translator, as well as director, that have enabled her to push beyond the access of welfare multiculturalism and contribute to the new styles of aesthetic multiculturalism, such as through her avant garde short films and female-centered mainstream features. Her assets are evident in how she brings her filmmaking background from Hong Kong and the United States, multi-language skills and diasporic connections. In particular, her proficiencies in Mandarin, Cantonese and Vietnamese have allowed her to translate across linguistic groups and impact industrial sectors. Her filmmaking background has also enriched the normatively white Australian media scene by pioneering new subject matter and roles that engage Australia in Asia. As filmmaker, she has injected new aesthetic styles by worlding Asia and fostering intercultural engagement. These new modes of Asian engagement transcend the stereotype Australian imaginary of Asia and introduce a multi-sited transnational polycentrism that pluralises both Asia and the West. This continues more markedly during the second and current phase of her Australian career.

4. Between China and Australia – the cultural broker

After *Traps*, Chan worked for two years as commissioner for the national film agency, the Australian Film Commission. This position set the foundation for the beginnings of her new role as a cultural gatekeeper in the industry. She released her second feature, *Little White Lies*, in 1996. Like *Traps*, the film was not a commercial success despite casting the Hollywood star Mimi Rogers. She decided to take a break from Australia to return to Hong Kong. Initially the trip was planned as a short visit to accompany her aging mother who wished to reunite with her relatives, but when Chan was offered the position as Senior Producer in charge of new business development for Salon Films, she took up the appointment (2001–2009) and remained in Hong Kong with her mother (Yue 2016).

Salon Films is Asia's premiere creative video agency. It produces and services feature films, commercial advertisements and short films.[3] Established in 1959, its collaborations include *The World of Suzie Wong* (dir. Quine 1960), *The Deer Hunter* (dir. Cimino 1978), *Indiana Jones and The Temple of Doom* (dir. Spielberg 1984), *Platoon* (dir. Stone 1986), *Cyclo* (dir. Tran 1995), *Shanghai Noon* (dir. Dey 2000), *The Ip Man Trilogy* (dir. Yip 2010-2015) and, *Bodyguards and Assassins* (dir. Chan 2009). During Chan's tenure, the agency also produced seminal films such as *Crouching Tiger, Hidden Dragon* (dir. Lee 2000), *In The Mood for Love* (dir. Wong Kar-wai 2000) and *The Forbidden Kingdom* (dir. Minkoff 2008). In addition to these titles, Chan was especially responsible for all the promotional videos for the 2008 Beijing Olympics. This was the period just before the rise of the global Chinese film industry (and its subsequent ascendency of the media conglomerates Dalian Wanda, Tencent and Alibaba) where Salon Films was a major broker for East–West and pan-Chinese film production. Chan gained significant contacts and deep insight into the then emergent Chinese industry. While in Hong Kong, she also co-founded Powerpool Investment, a business that specialises in financing company mergers in China and Hong Kong (Yue 2017). She brought with her these knowledge, skills and networks when she returned to Australia in 2010.

The second and current phase of Chan's Australian career began after her return from Hong Kong. In a span of seven short years, she successfully directed and produced at least three films and a major television series. She continues to mentor more titles by assisting filmmakers and establishing new businesses specialising in Chinese co-production. Through these capacities, she transitioned from a multicultural filmmaker to a cultural intermediary.

Cultural intermediaries are an occupational group of workers involved in the production of symbolic goods and services (Bourdieu 1984: 359). Included in this group are those who work in, for example, the industries of advertising, design, sales promotion and marketing. While these professions have been around since the nineteenth century, their role as cultural intermediaries emerged in recent decades with the rise of the cultural and creative economy. Cultural intermediaries exert cultural authority by defining taste and consumer desires. They are workers who come 'in-between' creative artists and consumers (Negus 2002: 504). By opening up the link between production and consumption and as gatekeepers, they show 'the interplay between these discrete moments in the life-cycle of cultural forms' (Nixon and du Gay 2002: 498). They construct value, frame how others in the supply chain (e.g., consumers and the marketplace) engage with the commodity (including goods, service, ideas), and affect what counts as legitimate (Smith Maguire and Matthews 2012). As 'the taste makers defining what counts as good taste and cool culture in today's marketplace' (Matthews and SmithMaguire 2014: 1), they thus 'shape both use values and exchange values' (Negus 2002: 504). Exemplary

[3]Film service companies facilitate film companies shooting on location in foreign countries by providing local production services such as interpreting local laws, permitting, partnering through incentives, providing crews and equipment rentals, and arranging hotels and transportation. With the current ascendency of the China film production market, the role of Salon Films in China has been diminished by new and bigger influential players such as China Film Company and Hengdian Studios.

in this group is the screen mediation work of someone like Chan, the film producer. The following exemplifies her cultural brokering characteristics following three core themes identified as central to research in this field: first, historicising the cultural intermediary profession; second, contextualising the concepts and specificities of practices, devices and dispositions that inform the work; and third, identifying the cultural, economic and political impacts of the work in the production and reproduction of culture (Matthews and Smith Maguire 2014: 7).

The changing profession of the co-producer is evident in policy and institutional developments. While film producers are among some of the professions that can be classified as belonging to the traditional sectors of film industry, the China–Australia co-production work that Chan is now involved in is a relatively new role, and one that draws on the diversity of work-related competencies she has accumulated across the whole of her career, which in turn has created new network assemblages. Australia began co-production in 1986 and signed its bilateral film treaty with China in 2006 (Yue 2014). The China treaty is Australia's first partnership in Asia. This treaty gives Australia preferential access to the Chinese market which has a foreign film quota of 38 films a year (Mumford 2017). Co-productions are considered domestic films and bypass the foreign film quota restrictions. At the time of signing the treaty, Australia was only the second country (after Canada) to have a bilateral film trade agreement with China.[4] From the beginning of the China treaty, Chan was central to brokering major film deals.

Chan brings her cross-cultural and multi-lingual skills, film and finance networks, and subjective dispositions to the role. She was one of the producers of *The Dragon Pearl* (dir. Andreacchio 2011), the first official Australia–China co-production. The film chronicles the friendship between a young Australian boy and a Chinese girl who met when accompanying their archaeologist-parents at an excavation site in China, and how they team up to investigate the legend of a dragon and its missing pearl. She helped Andreacchio negotiate the complexity of Sino-foreign co-production, in particular, navigate the guidelines on censorship and production administration from the State Administration of Press, Publication, Radio, Film and Television, and China Film Co-production Corporation (CFCC), the two main Chinese government agencies in charge of film co-production (Yue 2016). Although the Australian national film industry is a subsidised industry, directors are expected to secure matching commercial support for their films. Despite being billed as the first official Australia–China co-production, Andreacchio completed *The Dragon Pearl* with little Australian government support, not realising at that time that China was more interested in relationship-to-relationship contracts rather than deal-to-deal contracts (Wink 2012). Chan drew on her human and social capital by drawing on her industry experience and networks in China, and assisted not only with looking for Chinese financiers but also translation and language difficulties, two of the key obstacles in Sino-foreign co-productions. Her specialist knowledge of the Chinese film production system and audience taste is central to her role as a cultural gatekeeper. Similar to her earlier role as the film commissioner for the national film funding agency, her leadership here is also crucial to how subsidised film funding functions a policy tool for maintaining old and engineering new discourses in national cultural identity. She likens her co-

[4]China now has 13 other bilateral film partners including Singapore, France, Italy and the United Kingdom (CFCC 2014). Australia has ten film partner countries (Screen Australia 2017a).

production strategy to that of 'manufacturing a car rather than making a film': the product is an 'Australian export film ... with Australian creatives, Australian landscape, Australian technicians – 80 to 90 per cent shot and managed and crewed by Australians – with Chinese investment the major force behind the film' (Chan, cited in Maddox 2016). In diagnosing the product and the market, and interpreting consumer taste, she constructs cultural legitimacy for these films and their qualities (Matthews and Smith Maguire 2014: 9–10).

While she has always worked from her own production company, Darkroom Films – a small company that she founded in 1991 that specialises in creative development, financing and producing feature films and documentaries, especially across international joint ventures, it is significant to note that it is Chan herself and not her company that is mentioned in the film credits. This acknowledgement attests to her charisma. This is evident in the online photos that accompany her screen biography as well as her speaking appearances in the Australian film circuits. She is engaging when she speaks, and with long black hair and red lipstick, commands a stunning presence when she is on stage and in public. Indeed, her early acting career was buoyed by these traits. Chan also rose in status as a cultural broker through her specialist qualifications and the niche networks they open up, in particular, her Australian AFTRS film school pedigree and Hong Kong film capital are central to her pioneering status as a key player in the Australia–China co-production circuit. Through appearance and habitus, her embodied capital allows her to perform expertise, assert influence, and build a personal and recognisable brand.

In-between producing *The Dragon Pearl*, Chan also made and released her critically acclaimed third feature film, *33 Postcards* (2011), a story about a young orphan Chinese girl who has been dreaming for ten years to meet her Australian sponsor and finally gets the chance when her orphanage's choir group is invited to tour the country. Chan raised 64 per cent of the production budget from Chinese private financiers in less than a month after trying without success for 18 months in Australia, the United States and Europe (Dillon 2012: 95). This attests to the strength of her network and her capacity to create stories that are contemporary and appealing to both co-production partners. To attract the Chinese government and investors, she revised the defection script to show the Chinese in a favourable light, such as how Chinese authorities like the orphanage's matron also care about Mei Mei's welfare, and how Mei Mei decides to give up her asylum seeker application to stay in Australia and return with the choir group to China. Rather than viewing the script amendment as a compromise to the narrative, she revealed that these changes have allowed her to develop her characters with more depth and shade (Yue 2017). This practice provides insight into how the diaspora advantage is practised in a flexible mode that accommodates the political and ethical demands of neoliberal capitalism.

Throughout recent years, Chan continues to produce numerous films and mentor other directors. In John V. Soto's *The Gateway* (2018), a film about a physicist grieving over the loss of her husband who uses a revolutionary invention to bring him back to life, Chan helped Soto raise Chinese private equity through the media company Beijing Cheetah Yassa Culture, an incubator for media intellectual property she co-founded in 2015 (Yue 2017). She has also just completed the Australian shooting of *Butterfly Across the Seas*, China's biggest budget television series to be produced and shot outside of China. Through Opal Films International, a Perth-based company she started with Deirdre

Kitcher in 2015 that specialises in producing feature films as co-productions with partners from China and overseas, she is also developing *Dragon Eye*, a 3D feature film based on the Chinese classic story *Journey to the West*, and preparing to shoot her fourth feature film, *My Extraordinary Wedding*, a story about a Chinese wedding in Australia. Over the last 17 years in her capacity as producer, Chan's diaspora advantage has enabled her to raise more than US$260 million in intellectual property development and financing, including investment of US$30 million between China and Australia (Yue 2017).

The impact of her cultural intermediary work has set new standards for the Australian film industry. At an economic level, *The Dragon Pearl* and *33 Postcards* have been phenomenally successful, having been exhibited across 1100 screens in China (ICFF 2016). They have created a new genre form (the small budget independent film – a novel genre in an industry obsessed with blockbusters) and carved out a new commercial market for the ailing and minor Australian film industry, which only captured 7 per cent of the domestic box office market in 2016 (Screen Australia 2017b). China, on the other hand, has an audience size of more than 1.3 billion consumers, is the world's fastest growing market for box office sales, and has released 845 films in 2016 commanding 54 per cent of the domestic box office market (Dembla and Kapoor 2016). Not surprisingly, the Australian film industry is belatedly pivoting to China, with 14 films worth AUD $400 million currently in various stages of production (Screen Australia 2017c). Apart from production budget and ticket sales, the ancillary downstream effects are impactful too. For example, it is estimated that *At Last* (dir. Yiwei Liu), a Chinese film currently in pre-production about a Beijing couple who find themselves caught in an art heist while holidaying in Australia, will provide approximately two hundred jobs and inject AUD$10.8 million into the local Queensland economy (Keast 2017). Unlike the precarity of below the line film work, Australia China co-productions, in particular, have introduced new long-term career opportunities for Chinese Australian and bilingual film workers, including production managers, junior producers, young filmmakers, and actors, who will work as film leads but also undertake off-shore management roles (Opal Films International 2017). These impacts have challenged the ways power, privilege and patronage have been maintained by the traditions of normative Eurocentric Australian cinema and its white-centric elite professional class.

At a cultural and political level, Chan has also introduced new practices of intercultural engagement between Australia and China. Despite Australia's subordinate status in the bilateral partnership – what has been termed the junior partnership of minor transnationalism (Yue 2014) – the potential for genuine industry collaboration has resulted in the strategy of co-development rather than the hegemony of runaway production which has only benefitted the offshore subsidiaries of global Hollywood, where Chinese and Australians are involved as equal stakeholders from the very beginning of the script development and creative production process (Yue 2014). At this early stage of bilateralism, plots, however, tend to be risk averse, exploiting the stereotyped theme of cross-cultural marriage or friendship (e.g., *Tying the Knot* and *33 Postcards*), and/or through Australia and China as film-induced tourist locations (e.g., *My Extraordinary Wedding*). Nonetheless, co-productions are an ideal platform for cultural diplomacy. Rather than the one-way messaging of soft power, cultural diplomacy holds the potential to engage intercultural exchange as a two-way dialogic process of learning from and transforming one another (Lenczowski 2009). Cultural diplomacy projects usually take place through exchanges with the assumption that exchanges will create a network of influential people abroad that will tie them to their host country and appreciate their host country more due to their time spent there (Scott-Smith 2008). Co-productions are an example of such projects. Cultural residencies take the form of geographical, cultural and industrial immersion through months or year-long on-location shooting. These experiences have transformed the creatives involved, such as in the cast and crew of the Australia Singapore HBO-funded television series, *Serangoon Road* (dir. Barron 2013) (Yue, in press). Indeed, studies have shown that Asian and Australian artists who have participated in cultural residencies have developed cosmopolitan capacities through new networks of sharing and dialogue (Roesler 2015). As Kitcher, Chan's business partner, has lauded, '[Chan] has done a magnificent job on the cross-cultural differences between not just Australia and China but also Hong Kong and mainland China' (Quoted in George 2015).

5. Conclusion

This paper has critically developed the diaspora advantage as a new conceptual approach to introduce and situate the screen career of Pauline Chan, Australia's most prolific and innovative Chinese director and producer. The diaspora advantage is characterised by mobility rather than culturalism and optimises the capacity to leverage transnational skills, resources and networks, especially across relationships, partnerships and collaborations between home and hostlands. Mobility is explicitly evident in Chan's personal and professional histories of migration, first from Vietnam and then to Hong Kong, America and Australia, and back again to Hong Kong and China, and now, in her constant travels across these continents in her expanded role as a joint venture broker. Mobility is also implicitly evident in the way she deftly navigates changing screen and cultural policy regimes to introduce new developments in film style and industrial mode.

This paper has also critically elaborated various features of Chan's diasporic advantage including her family history of filmmaking; multi-lingual skills; niche networks created from her specialist training in Australia's premiere film school; Hong Kong and Chinese film capital; and her subjective disposition as a charismatic and visionary cultural pioneer. Through her diaspora advantage, she has increased filmmaking capacity with creative business ventures that have tapped into the growing cultural economies of Asia in general and China in particular, forging a new regional pathway for the Australian national film sector, its directors and cultural workers.

Central to her diaspora advantage is her transformation from a multicultural filmmaker to a cultural intermediary. While she gained entry into the industry through the access afforded by welfare multiculturalism, she used this opportunity to introduce new ways of telling stories about Asia and Asians. In her early career as actress, film researcher and script translator, she challenged the stereotyped representation of Asians by assisting established Anglo Australian male filmmakers make films in Asia and about Asians. As a young director, she created novel styles with her experimental, avant-garde and female-centred films that allowed her to introduce an aesthetic multiculturalism informed by a polycentric practice that 'worlds' and re-engages Asia and Australia. Her current leadership as a cultural broker continues this aesthetic engagement by forging revolutionary co-development and joint venture strategies for film co-production. She has become the cultural gatekeeper for Australian cinema eyeing Asia as the world's biggest media entertainment market, and instituted new genres and networks that have the potential to build literacy and competency across Asia and Australia. Through these roles, her diaspora advantage has reconfigured the Asia Australian cultural imaginary from the ghettos of minority cinema to a transnational cultural form supported by a global network of flexible and smart creatives.

The diaspora advantage is a form of embodied agency and a practice of cooperation embedded in unequal transnational power structures. As embodied agency, it builds on the deployment and accrual of career capital diversity such as those that influence and impact motivational, human and social capitals. These skill-set domains expand multiculturalism's nominal focus on cultural diversity and difference by focusing on individual work-related competencies across the whole of a career. While these competencies are self-optimised to reflect current neoliberal accumulation strategies, for diasporic subjects to survive and adapt in new host countries, these strategies have the potential to turn migrant disadvantage into advantage, such as in the earlier stereotyping and the latter ascendency of Chan's career. As a practice of cooperation, the diaspora advantage furnishes the potential to create new transnational assemblages that can transgress official cultural forms, such as through the film partnerships brokered by Chan. Chan's above the line role as a cultural intermediary leader should not deflect from how power is transacted in the material intersections of such exchanges. Her reflection on her own amendment to the film script of *33 Postcards* calls to task the equity of bilateral cooperation and the ethics at stake for a minor stakeholder in a junior partnership. These minoritisations are more amplified for below the line workers, such as those in China on joint Hollywood film sets where even meal canteens are stratified according to nationalities, such as lunch boxes for the Chinese and buffet spreads for the Americans (Kokas 2017). In creating productive and permanent cultural forms, the diaspora advantage is also an assemblage to expose such unequal power relations.

Acknowledgements

I would like to thank Dan Edwards for his research assistance, Pauline Chan for her generosity and time with the interviews and the editors and anonymous referees for their insightful comments which have helped to strengthen the conceptual framing around the diaspora advantage. Any mistakes are solely my own.

Disclosure statement

No potential conflict of interest was reported by the authors.

Funding

This project received funding from the Australian Research Council Discovery Project DP160100304.

References

Amenta, P. and Millar, C. 1986. *Sword of Honour.* 7 Network. Simpson Le Mesurier Films. Australia.

Andreacchio, M. 2011. *The Dragon Pearl.* AMPCO Films. Hengdian World Studios. Australia/China.

Ang, I., Tambieh, Y. and Mar, P. 2015. *Smart Engagement with Asia: Leveraging Language, Research and Culture.* Report for the Australian Council of Learned Academies. Available online at https://acola.org.au/wp/ (accessed 13 February 2017).

Asian Australian Cinema database. 2012. Available online at http://asianaustraliancinema.org/ (accessed 12 February 2017).

Barron, P. 2013. *Serangoon Road.* HBO Asia and Australian Broadcasting Corporation. Singapore and Australia.

Bennett, G. and Cox, P. 1985. *Winners.* Film Finances. South Australian Film Corporation. Australia.

Beresford, B. 1997. *Paradise Road.* Australia: Samson Productions Pty. Ltd.

Bourdieu, P. 1984. *Distinction: A Social Critique of the Judgement of Taste.* New York: Routledge.

Borjas, G. J. 1989. 'Economic Theory and International migration'. *International Migration Review* 23, 457–85.

Brubaker, R. 2005. 'The "Diaspora" diaspora'. *Ethnic and Racial Studies* 28:1, 1–19.

Burstall, T. 1981. *Attack Force Z.* Australian Film Commission. Australia.

Cameron, K. 1989. *Bangkok Hilton.* Kennedy Miller Productions. Australia.

Carr, A. 1989. *Sword of the Bushido.* John Lamond Motion Picture Enterprises. Australia.

Carment, D. and Sadjed, A. 2017. 'Conclusion: Diasporas as Cultures of Cooperation'. In David Carment and Ariane Sadjed (eds), *Diaspora as Cultures of Cooperation: Global and Local Perspectives.* London: Palgrave, 261–72.

Carter, R. 1998. *The Sugar Factory.* Imagine Films Entertainment. Australia.

Chan, P. 1990a. *The Space between the Door.* Australian Film and Television School. Australia.

Chan, P. 1990b. *Hang Up.* Australian Film and Television School. Australia.

Chan, P. 1991. *Dusty Hearts.* Australian Film and Television School. Australia.

Chan, P. 1994. *Traps.* J. McElroy Holdings. Australia.

Chan, P. 1996. *Little White Lies.* Film Queensland. John Sexton Productions. Australia.

Chan, T. 2009. *Bodyguards and Assassins (dir.).* Hong Kong, China: Beijing Poly-bona Film Publishing Company.

Chan, P. 2011. *33 Postcards.* Portal Pictures. Zhejiang Hengdian Film Production. Australia/China.

China Film Co-Production Corporation (CFCC). 2014. 'Chinese-Foreign Film Co-Production Agreements'. Available online at http://www.cfcc-film.com.cn/policeg/content/id/2.html (accessed 12 February 2017).

Cimino, M. 1978. The *Deer Hunter.* EMI Films. Universal Pictures. USA.

Collier, S. J. and Ong, A. 2005. 'Global Assemblages, Anthropological Problems'. In Aihwa Ong and Stephen J. Collier (eds), *Global Assemblages. Technology, Politics, and Ethics as Anthropological Problems.* Malden, MA: Blackwell, 3–21.

Cope, B., Kalantzis, M. and Ziguras, C. 2003. *Multimedia, Multiculturalism and the Arts.* Sydney: Australia Council.

Crombie, D. 1989. *The Saint: Fear in the Fun Park.* 7 Network. Australia.

Davis, E. 1975. *That Lady from Peking.* Commonwealth United Entertainment. Australia.

Dembla, P. and Kapoor, S. 2016. 'Report: Film Industry in China', August, ICA Institute. Available online at http://dga.kennesaw.edu/ica/ (accessed 30 April 2017).

Department of Communication and the Arts (DCA). 1994. *Creative nation: commonwealth cultural policy, October* 1994. Available online at http://www.nla.gov.au/creative.nation/contents.html (accessed 26 February 2005).

Dermody, S. M. 1992. *Breathing Under Water.* Periscope Productions. Australia.
Dey, T. 2000. *Shanghai Noon.* Touchstone Pictures. USA.
Dillon, J. 2012. 'Letter to a Neighbour: Pauline Chan on Crossing Cultural Lines Through Film'. *Metro Magazine* 173, 94–6.
Duigan, J. 1982. *Far East.* Alfred Road Productions. Australia.
Duigan, J. and Noonan, C. 1987. *Vietnam.* Kennedy Miller Productions. Australia.
Fish, S. 1997. 'Boutique Multiculturalism, or Why Liberals Are Incapable of Thinking About Hate Speech'. *Critical Inquiry* 23:2, 378–95.
Fitzgerald, J. and Chau, W. 2014. *International Cultural Engagements among Australians of Pacific Islands and Asian Descent: A Preliminary Research Report*, Report for the Australian Council of Learned Academies. Available online at http://acola.org.au/ index.php/saf03-contributing-reports (accessed 12 February 2017).
George, S. 2015. 'Beijing Film Market popular with Australian producers' 16 April, *Screen Daily.* Available online at http://www.screendaily.com/news/beijing-film-market-popular-with-australian-producers-/5086632.article (accessed 30 April 2017).
G.P. 1989–1996. Roadshow Coote and Carroll. Australia.
Grass Roots. 2000–2003. Australian Broadcasting Corporation. Australia.
Grenville, K. 1986. *Dreamhouse.* Brisbane: University of Queensland Press.
Gunew, S. and Rizvi, F. 1994. *Culture, Difference and the Arts.* St Leonards, NSW: Allen and Unwin.
Hage, G. 1998. *White Nation: Fantasies of White Supremacy in a Multicultural Society.* Sydney: Pluto Press.
Hall, S. 1990. 'Cultural Identity and Diaspora', In Jonathan Rutherford (ed), *Identity, Community, Culture, Difference.* London: Lawrence and Wishart, 222–237.
Hawkins, G. 1993. *From Nimbin to Mardi Gras: Constructing Community Arts.* St Leonards, NSW: Allen & Unwin.
Holden, S. 1995. 'No Wonder the Guests are Nervous', 1 December, *New York Times.* Available online at http://www.nytimes.com/movie/review?res=980DEFDA1139F932A35751C1A96395 8260 (accessed 3 June 2017).
Holden, J. 2013. *Influence and Attraction: Culture and the Race for Soft Power in the 21st Century.* London: British Council/ Demos. Available online at http://www.britishcouncil.org/press/ changing-soft- power-report (accessed 12 February 2017).
Honig, B., Drori, I. and Carmichael, B. (eds). 2010. *Transnational and Immigrant Entrepreneurship in a Globalized World.* Toronto: University of Toronto Press.
Hoole, D. 1982. *Storm Raiders.* Hoole-McCoy Films, Australia.
International Chinese Film Festival (ICFF). 2016. 'Pauline Chan Australian Director and Producer'. Available online at http://www.icff.cc/icff2016/pauline-chan/ (accessed 15 May 2017).
Jeffrey, T. 1979. *The Odd Angry Shot.* Samson Productions Pty. Ltd. Australia.
Jupp, J. 1996. *Understanding Australian Multiculturalism.* Canberra: Australian Govt. Pub. Service.
Keast, J. 2017. 'Chinese-Australian co-pro "At Last" to shoot in Queensland', *Intermedia*, 21 April. Available online at http://if.com.au/2017/04/21/article/Chinese-Australian-co-pro-At-Last-to-shoot-in-Queensland/ULUGMFARXU.html (accessed 30 April 2017).
Khoo, O., Smaill, B. and Yue, A. 2013. *Transnational Australian Cinema: Ethics in the Asian Diasporas.* Lanham: Lexington Books.
Kokas, A. 2017. *Hollywood Made in China: What is At Stake?* Berkeley, CA: University of California Press.
Law, C. 1996. *Floating Life.* Hibiscus Films. Southern Star Entertainment. Australia.
Lee, A. 2000. *Crouching Tiger, Hidden Dragon.* Asian Union Film and Entertainment. China Film Co-Production Corporation, Columbia Pictures Film Production Asia. USA/China/Hong Kong.
Lenczowski, J. 2009. 'Cultural Diplomacy, Political Influence, and Integrated Strategy'. In L. Michael Waller (ed). *Strategic Influence: Public Diplomacy, Counter Propaganda, and Political Warfare.* Washington, DC: Institute of World Politics Press, 74–99.
Liu, H. 2012. 'Beyond a Revisionist Turn: Networks, State and the Changing Dynamics of Diasporic Chinese entrepreneurship'. *China: An International Journal* 10:3, 20–42.

Maddox, G. 2016. 'Pauline Chan's wise advice for filmmakers looking for a break: 走向 中国夢', *The Sydney Morning Herald*, 7 December. Available online at http://www.smh.com.au/entertainment/movies/pauline-chans-wise-advice-for-filmmakers-looking-for-a-break--20161124-gsww0 h.html (accessed 30 April 2017).
Matthews, J. and Maguire, J. S. 2014. 'Introduction: Thinking Cultural with Cultural Intermediaries'. In Julian Matthews and Jennifer Smith Maguire (eds), *The Cultural Intermediaries Reader*. Los Angeles, London & New Delhi: Sage Publications, 1–11.
McCoy, J. 1976. *In Search of Tubular Swells*. Hoole-McCoy Films. Australia.
McCoy, J. 1980. *Kongs Island*. Hoole-McCoy Films. Australia.
McGregor, J. 2014. 'Sentimentality of Speculation? Diaspora Investment, Crisis Economics and Urban transformation'. *Geoforum; Journal of Physical, Human, and Regional Geosciences* 56, 172–81.
McKeown, A. 2000. 'From Opium Farmer to Astronaut: A Global History of Diasporic Chinese Business'. *Diaspora: A Journal of Transnational Studies* 9:3, 317–60.
Miller, G. 1979–2015. *Mad Max* franchise. Kennedy Miller. Australia.
Miller, G. 2006–2011. *Happy Feet* franchise. Kennedy Miller. Australia.
Minkoff, R. 2008. *The Forbidden Kingdom*. China Film Co-Production Corporation. Huayi Brothers Media. Hong Kong/China.
Mumford, G. 2017. 'China's Hollywood film quota to expand after Trump trade deal', 12 April. Available online at https://www.theguardian.com/film/2017/apr/12/trump-xi-trade-talks-china-hollywood-film-quota (accessed 30 April 2017).
Negus, K. 2002. 'The Work of Cultural Intermediaries and the Enduring Distance Between Production and Consumption'. *Cultural Studies* 16:4, 501–15.
Nixon, S. and Gay, P. D. 2002. 'Who Needs Cultural Intermediaries?' *Cultural Studies* 16:4, 495–500.
Ong, A. and Nonini, D. (eds). 1997. *Ungrounded Empires: The Cultural Politics of Modern Chinese Transnationalism*. New York: Routledge.
Opal Films International. 2017. 'Employment Opportunities'. Available online at http://www.opalfilms.net/jobs.html (accessed 30 June 2017).
O'Regan, T. 1996. *Australian National Cinema*. London: Routledge.
Prowse, A. 1989. *Driving Force*. Eastern Film Management Corporation. Australia.
Quayson, A. 2013. *A Companion to Diaspora and Transnationalism*. Hoboken: Wiley.
Quine, R. 1960. *The World of Suzie Wong*. World Enterprises. USA.
Rizvi, F., Louie, K. and Evans, J. 2016. *Australia's Diaspora Advantage: Realising the Potential for Building Transnational Business Networks with Asia*. Melbourne: Australian Council of Learned Academies.
Romero, E. 1989. *A Case of Honour*. Eastern Film Management Corporation. Australia.
Rösler, B. 2015. 'The Case of Asialink's Arts Residency Program: Towards a Critical Cosmopolitan Approach to Cultural diplomacy'. *International Journal of Cultural Policy* 21:4, 463–77.
Said, E. 1983. *The World, the Text, and the Critic*. Cambridge, MA: Harvard University Press.
Sangita, S. 2013. 'The Effect of Diasporic Business Networks on International Trade Flows'. *Review of International Economics* 21:2, 266–80.
Santiago, C. H. 1987. *Killer Instinct*. Eastern Film Management Corporation. Australia.
Schultz, C. 1989. *Cassidy*. Five Arrows Film. Australia.
Scott-Smith, G. 2008. 'Mapping the Undefinable: Some Thoughts on the Relevance of Exchange Programs Within International Relations Theory'. *Annals of the American Academy of Political and Social Science* 16, 1743–195.
Screen Australia. 2016. *Seeing Ourselves: Reflections on Diversity in Australian TV drama*. Sydney, Screen Australia.
Screen Australia. 2017a. 'Partner Countries'. Available online at https://www.screenaustralia.gov.au/funding-and-support/co-production-program/partner-countries (accessed 12 February 2017).
Screen Australia. 2017b. 'Cinema Industry Trends'. Available online at https://www.screenaustralia.gov.au/fact-finders/cinema/industry-trends/films-screened (accessed 30 April 2017).

Screen Australia. 2017c. 'New Australian-Chinese co-production feature announced', 20 April. Available online at https://www.screenaustralia.gov.au/sa/media-centre/news/2017/mr-170420-australian-chinese-copro (accessed 30 May 2017).

Semyonov, M. and Gorodzeisky, A. 2008. 'Labour Migration, Remittances and the Well-Being of Households in the Philippines'. *Population Research and Policy Review* 27:5, 619–38.

Smith Maguire, J. and Matthews, J. 2012. 'Are We All Cultural Intermediaries Now? An Introduction to Cultural Intermediaries in Context'. *European Journal of Cultural Studies* 15:5, 551–62.

Soto, J. V. 2018. *The Gateway*. Filmscope Entertainment. Australia.

Spielberg, S. 1984. *Indiana Jones and The Temple of Doom*. Paramount Pictures. Lucasfilm. USA.

Stone, O. 1986. *Platoon*. Hemdale. USA.

Stratton, D. 1994. 'Traps', *Variety*, 6 June. Available online at http://variety.com/1994/film/reviews/traps-1200437684/ (accessed 3 June 2017).

Thomas, K. 1995. 'Movie Review: "Traps": Passion and Honesty Get Lost in a Tangled Web', *Los Angeles Times*, 1 December. Available online at http://articles.latimes.com/1995-12-01/entertainment/ca-9160_1_michael-duffield (accessed 30 June 2017).

Tran, A. H. 1993. *The Scent of the Green Papaya*. Les Productions Lazennec. France.

Tran, A. H. 1995. *Cyclo*. Canal. France.

Trenchard-Smith, B. 1975. *The Man from Hong Kong*. Golden Harvest. Australia/Hong Kong.

Trenchard-Smith, B. 1976. *Death Cheaters*, Brian Trenchard-Smith Productions. Australia.

Trenchard-Smith, B. 1989. *The Siege of Firebase Gloria*. Eastern Film Management Corporation. Australia.

Turnbull, S. and Collins, F. 2001. 'Old Dogs, New Tricks: Beyond Simpson Le Mesurier, Crime-Comedy and the Telemovie Series'. *Media International Australia Incorporating Culture and Policy* 100, 33–48.

Viviani, N. 1999. 'Asian Migration: Human Rights, Human Wrongs, Citizenship and Multiculturalism'. *Australian Cultural History* 18, 57–71.

Wallace, S. 1990. *Blood Oath*. Blood Oath Productions. Australia.

Wang, G. 1993. 'Greater China and the Chinese Overseas'. *The China Quarterly* 136, 926–48.

Weir, P. 1982. *The Year of Living Dangerously*. McElroy and McElroy. Australia.

Wilson, R. and Connery, C. L. (eds). 2007. *The Worlding Project: Doing Cultural Studies in the Era of Globalization*. Berkeley, CA: North Atlantic Books.

Wink, M. 2012. *Finding The Dragon Pearl: Australia-China Co-productions in the 'Golden Age' of Chinese Film*. MA thesis, Dept of Public Policy, Central European University. Available online: www.etd.ceu.hu/2012/wink_malinda.pdf (Accessed 12 Feb 2017).

Wong, K-w. 2000. *In The Mood for Love*. Block 2 Pictures. Hong Kong.

Yip, W. 2010–2015. *The Ip Man Trilogy*. China Film Co-Production Corporation. Hong Kong/China.

Yue, A. 2014. 'Contemporary Sinophone Cinema: Australia-China Co-Productions'. In Audrey Yue and Olivia Khoo (eds), *Sinophone Cinemas*. London: Palgrave, 185–202.

Yue, A. 2016. Interview with Pauline Chan. 12 December. Sydney.

Yue, A. 2017. Interview with Pauline Chan. 7 March 2017. Sydney.

Yue, A. in press. '*Serangoon Road*: The Convergent Culture of Minor Transnationalism'. In Felicity Collins, Jane Landman and Susan Bye (eds), *The Wiley Blackwell Companion to Australian Cinema*. London: Blackwell.

Yue, A. and Khan, R. 2014. 'Accounting for Multiculturalism: The Utility of Cultural Indicators and the Politics of Diversity and Participation', *Conjunctions: Transdisciplinary Journal of Cultural Participation* 1:1, 1–28. Available online at http://www.conjunctions-tjcp.com/article/view/18600

Zikic, J. 2015. "Skilled Migrants' Career Capital as a Source of Competitive Advantage: Implications for Strategic HRM'. *The International Journal of Human Resource Management* 26:10, 1360–81.

7 The paradoxes of creativity in Guangzhou, China's wholesale market for fast fashion

Nellie Chu

ABSTRACT
In Guangzhou's fast fashion sector, creativity operates as practices in boundary-making, which emerge in spaces within the blurred boundaries that delineate original and copy production. Using the Xi Fang Hang market as a case study, I demonstrate how the quick turnover of fast fashion commodities compels different groups of market participants to claim contesting definitions and practices of creativity. While building managers and wealthy entrepreneurs mobilise techniques of rent extraction and claim originality as rightful sources of creativity, less established migrant entrepreneurs use design copying as a tool for market survival. With limited resources and formal education in fashion and merchandising, migrants claim success in delivering the right styles and trends at the right time and in keeping their businesses afloat. Together, these competing practices constitute what I call 'paradoxes of creativity', dynamics that highlight creativity as a fluid cultural category that is always subject to tensions and contestations.

In the heart of Guangzhou's historic Yuexiu district, migrant entrepreneurs from all regions of China swarm through the hallways of Xi Fang Hang, an internationally recognised wholesale market for low-cost garments. They are members of China's 'floating population', the over 280 million undocumented and internally displaced migrants from the nation's countryside. According to the *hukou* system of population control, rural migrants are legally excluded from urban citizenship, and are thus denied access to state-sponsored services, including housing, education and health care, in Guangzhou. Inside this wholesale market, thousands of tiny stalls separated by simple steel frames are jammed beside each other, forming narrow rows along massive market floors. Nearly every individual stall is leased to a small-scale migrant entrepreneur. Lured by the prospects of fast and easy money, these migrant entrepreneurs move to Guangzhou and forge ties with transnational agents from South Korea, Hong Kong and countries across Southeast Asia and Africa. These transnational intermediaries purchase unbranded, ready-to-wear garments in bulk before the items are sent on and resold in retail outlets and secondary wholesale markets throughout West Africa, the Middle East, East Asia, Latin America and Southeast Asia. Collectively,

Chinese migrants' low-wage and precarious labour sustains the global commodity chains for fast fashion. Fast fashion refers to the small-scale, flexible and just-in-time delivery of designer-inspired garments and accessories. It is a contemporary mode of transnational production that relies primarily on the outsourcing of labour and manufacturing capabilities in places across the Global South (Horning 2011; Park 2012; Chu 2016; Moon 2017). This fashion sector emphasises speedy and intensive design work in the production of low-cost garments and accessories in order to facilitate the quick turnover of stylistic designs and trends (Raustiala and Sprigman 2006).

Limited in terms of financial resources and formal education in fashion and merchandising, Chinese migrant entrepreneurs rely on the ubiquitous practice of design copying, a key feature in the fast fashion sector. This practice enables market participants to keep pace with the rapid turnover of new trends as well as the fierce competition for fast money. Unlike designers, migrant entrepreneurs have limited social mobility, yet they take enormous financial risks in running stalls in Xi Fang Hang. New styles flood the market stalls nearly every week. Stalls frequently go out of business, and are often filled by a group of new owners nearly every year. Disputes among competing bosses arise, often revolving around claims related to design copying.

One female buyer who frequented the market described a confrontation that erupted when a wholesaler was fined by one of the building managers for selling a counterfeit garment. Apparently, a pattern used in one of her garments closely resembled a design trademarked by an internationally recognised luxury brand. The wholesaler disputed this charge, claiming that her garment was an original design. The observer remarked, 'Of course, [the dispute] had to do with money – kickbacks, really. We [as outside observers] don't know the types of collusive relationships and business interests that are tied to their monthly collections of rent.' Her reference to kickbacks implied a web of social relationships that structured the ways in which stalls and commercial spaces within the building were allotted and sub-leased. For those who regularly visit the market, where disputes over design copying and counterfeiting flare up on a regular basis, this particular altercation unmasked the deepening divisions in access to wealth and real estate that characterise this commercial space.

This essay examines how building managers, wealthy local bosses, and small-scale migrant entrepreneurs in Guangzhou, south China, variously exploit and sustain the ambiguities and paradoxes that blur the categories of creativity and design copying in order to negotiate the widening divisions in wealth and market access across the supply chains for fast fashion. Because of its emphasis on consumer choice and speed, creative output in this fashion sector relies on the practice of design copying to the extent that it is often difficult to distinguish an original from a copy design.[1] In effect, ambiguities over the definitions of creativity and design copying, as I show, serve as regulatory functions over the ongoing and speculative production of marketspaces and fashion trends.

Specifically, I analyse the work of wealthy local bosses, building managers and migrant entrepreneurs in regulating and keeping pace with the ongoing turnover of new styles and trends, as well as the marketspaces and market rhythms that are linked to these practices.

[1]In his article, Rob Horning (2011) demonstrates how the democratisation of fashion via the fast fashion business model produces the effect of creativity among mass consumers. He states, 'Consumers are invited to be expressive rather than imitative with the goods, to participate more directly with fashion ... The more clothes come in, the more creative we can be.'

Drawing from Raustiala and Sprigman's (2006) notion, 'the piracy paradox', this essay elaborates on what I call 'the paradoxes of creativity'. By 'paradoxes of creativity', I mean the market contradictions that emerge within the blurred boundaries that delineate original and copy production. In fast fashion, creativity is manifest in practices of boundary-making, which produce the uneven rhythms and spaces that link up with the industry's rapid turnover of trends. The lines that define original and copy, as well as fashion and non-fashion, are constantly contested and redrawn. As Star and Griesemer (1989: 393) state:

> Boundary objects are objects which are both plastic enough to adapt to local needs and constraints of the several parties employing them, yet robust enough to maintain a common identity across sites. They may be abstract or concrete. They have different meanings in different social worlds but their structure is common enough to more than one world to make them recognisable, a means of translation. The creation and management of boundary objects is key in developing and maintaining coherence across intersecting social worlds.

Taking Star and Griesemer's definition, I view fast fashion commodities as boundary objects that straddle the material and discursive worlds of original design and design copying. It is within the fluid boundaries of inventiveness and copy that regulatory practices emerge over who can extract profits from whom, and the ways in which these extractive activities can be carried out by building managers, migrant entrepreneurs and competing bosses. In this transnational market for low-cost goods, competing participants in the city's fast fashion sector speculate on the amount of profits that one can make through the ubiquitous practice of 'buying low and selling high'. I recount ethnographic examples that illustrate the regulatory activities that shape Chinese migrants' experiences of market competition. Market participants exploit and sustain the spatiotemporal unevenness and aesthetic ambiguities that result from the ongoing turnover of fast fashion in the following ways: (1) attempts by building managers to extract rent by controlling the rapid turnover of marketspaces; (2) migrant entrepreneurs' struggles in synchronising the mass manufacture of garments with the ongoing turnover of new styles; and (3) the contested claims to originality and inventiveness which wealthy local bosses and migrant entrepreneurs assert vis-à-vis one another. These market dynamics challenge conventional definitions of creativity simply as forms of social capital possessed and cultivated by those who have them, contrasted with those who do not. As a relational dynamic with its own inherent tensions and contradictions, creativity is a fluid and unstable category whose cultural meanings are highly contested.

In his theory of the creative class, Richard Florida (2002, 2005, 2011) expands the notion of creativity beyond the idea of aesthetic originality and applies the term in other areas of social life such as urban lifestyles, innovation economies, and entrepreneurship. To be sure, market participants in Xi Fang Hang use creativity both in this broader entrepreneurial sense as well as in the intellectual property sense, so as to position themselves in the marketplace vis-à-vis one another. Such competing discourses of creativity signal a relational struggle among migrant entrepreneurs in gaining market access and accumulating profits while displacing market risks to other suppliers across the commodity chains. Building managers and wealthy entrepreneurs mobilise techniques of rent extraction, quality control, and labour discipline under the guise of 'creativity' in order to control and slow down the rapid turnover of commodities, people and marketspaces. These techniques include requiring the seasonal upscaling of designer showrooms by less established migrant entrepreneurs, while at the same time appropriating their designs in order to position themselves vis-à-vis their market competitors along hierarchies of quality and value. In doing so, wealthier bosses who dominate the supply chains for fast fashion assert their designs as rightful sources of creativity. They claim that they produce original, high-quality clothing that is inspiring and inventive enough to generate and sustain a profitable market niche before those designs are replaced by new trends.

In contrast, less established and less wealthy entrepreneurs understand the necessity of design copying for market survival, as they aspire to join the ranks of the creative classes. Their view mirrors what Kedron Thomas (2016) writes: '[In fashion], copying and appropriation are essential to engaging in a creative process and to making a complete [stylistic] look' (10). Rather than claiming originality as a source of their creativity, migrant entrepreneurs are concerned with catching up with the rapid and ongoing turnover of fashion trends. As another stall owner in the market describes, 'Bigger bosses have the education and money to be successful [in this business]. For us, success comes from having the intuition and foresight to sell the right style at the right time.' In short, unpredictable market dynamics produce sites of ongoing disputes as well as underlying forces of competition.

Contestations characteristic of Guangzhou's fast fashion industry mask the class-based divisions among building managers, wealthy local bosses, and migrant entrepreneurs. These divisions impose a double displacement among migrant entrepreneurs who must struggle to keep up with flows of money and commodities in order to sustain their businesses. They must compete with one another in order to control and to slow down the rapid and seasonal turnover of marketspaces and stylistic trends. Their efforts, however, inadvertently deepen the social divisions in wealth accumulation and market access, since building managers and wealthier bosses exploit the moments of contestation among migrant entrepreneurs through various rent-seeking activities. Seeking returns on their property investments in the building, wealthy managers and bosses rely on the ongoing flows of lessees, clients, money and commodities. Their business interests lie in direct contradiction with those of the migrant entrepreneurs.

Despite the successes of popular media and state propaganda in popularising creativity, or *chuangyi* (创意), within China's mainstream discourse, the term remains an ambiguous and abstract concept, the essential characteristics of which few market participants can adequately pin down (Pang 2012). Indeed, the fine line that distinguishes creativity from design copying remains a central tension in the day-to-day business of fast fashion. An ethnographic analysis of the dynamic practices among competing groups of market participants lends critical insights into the productive tensions between original and copied fashion designs in the creation of new trends. It also sheds light on the social inequalities, design practices and ambiguous discourses that such tensions engender. In Xi Fang Hang, creativity is generally gauged by the level of newness and appeal a product brings to the consumer-driven market in a timely manner. Specifically, newness is produced through a combination of original designs and copied designs appropriated from past fashion trends. The proportion of what is original and what is copied differs by season, and is difficult to predict and measure. As a stall-owner in Xi Fang Hang explains, 'Everyone copies and borrows in this market. *Chuangyi* (creativity) comes from having an eye and a *feel* for what styles will be in fashion.' For this wholesaler, creativity stems from having an intuition for market turnovers, and delivering the right trend at the right time.

In turn, the interplay between original designs and copy designs within Guangzhou's fast fashion market shapes Chinese migrants' experiences of 'bosshood' and other creative endeavours, which in recent years have been politically mobilised under the banners of risk-taking entrepreneurship (*chuang* 闯) and creativity (*chuangyi*).[2] Popular discourses of *chuangyi* emerge at a contemporary moment when the politicisation of class-based inequalities and collective labour under Maoism are no longer used by migrant labourers to describe their experiences of work and self-employment (Chumley 2016). Instead, migrant entrepreneurs in Guangzhou employ the language of *chuangyi* to describe the sense of entrepreneurial freedom they aspire to attain in their business and work lives. Migrants quickly learn, however, that their entrepreneurial freedom is conditioned by the cyclical turnover of fashion trends, which coincides with the speculative pressures of Guangzhou's real estate market, as evidenced by the seasonal rise of rents within the fashion markets. In the sections that follow, I trace how friction between the material and discursive practices of creativity and copying plays out through speculation on the marketspaces and temporalities within the low-cost fashion markets in Guangzhou. The ethnographic vignettes that follow narrate how ambiguities between originality and copying link up with the economies of real estate speculation, policing and rent-extraction. These tensions are markedly demonstrated in Guangzhou's Xi Fang Hang, where stall and boutique owners mobilise *chuangyi* as a discursive resource in their attempts to occupy marketspaces and to control market rhythms. Through the discourse of *chuangyi*, migrant entrepreneurs compete to gain access to coveted market niches through the 'flipping' (*chao*) or speculation of time and marketspaces. The speedy and hyper-competitive rhythms of the fast fashion industry induce building managers and migrant entrepreneurs to 'fix' or control the rapid turnover of designs, workers, commodities and marketspaces, while limiting market access to their competitors (Harvey 2001). As geographer David Harvey (2001) elaborates, the circulation of money, labourers and commodities relies on stabilising or fixing investments onto land in order to create new landscapes amenable for capital accumulation. Here, I show how cultural categories covering competing definitions and practices of creativity also serve as sites of market regulation and control. The circulation of money, commodities and marketspaces exacerbates competition among market participants who assert competing claims over their rightful sources of originality, inventiveness and entrepreneurial success.

Politics of creativity and newness in the Xi Fang Hang fashion market

While social scientists have written extensively on the link between the creative economy and fashion, their studies have tended to focus on branding and intellectual property rights in the social construction of logos and their counterfeits (Coombe 1998; Vann 2006; Lin 2011; Nakassis 2013; Thomas 2012, 2016). These scholars have underscored how people in different regions of the world hold historically distinct understandings of creativity, originality, and their relationships to copies and fakes (Vann 2006; Lin 2011; Thomas 2016). Other scholars have insightfully pointed out that the ongoing tension or 'friction' between practices of creativity and copying operates as a generative force that yields the ongoing

[2]In Chinese, creativity (*chuangyi*) and taking risks (*chuang*) use two separate meanings of *chuang*, and are thus denoted by different characters.

production of 'newness' within creative industries such as art, digital media, and fashion (Tsing 2005; Pang 2012; Moon 2014).[3]

Specifically, in fashion, the creation of styles must be constantly replaced by the incoming flow of new trends (Mason 2008; English 2013).[4] As Laikwan Pang (2012) writes, within the logic of intellectual property law, branded commodities must be constantly displaced by their reproductions, marked by both aesthetic likeness and difference, in order for the cultural categories of authenticity and counterfeit to remain ideologically stable (194). Likewise, in her discussion on fashion trends and self-styling, Lily Chumley (2016) highlights the ways in which students within Beijing's burgeoning art schools display their aesthetic fluidity and creativity by dressing and performing stylistic differences but within the rigid structural dynamics of aesthetic and political containment, as manifested in teacher–student relationships, state propaganda and the global art markets. While cultural theorists Pang and Chumley point to the widening social inequalities masked by these oppositions, legal scholars Raustiala and Sprigman (2006) write in praise of such paradoxes by highlighting the creative and productive energies generated by the ongoing turnover of fashion trends. They argue that design copying paradoxically benefits the creative capacities of fashion designers and helps to reinforce intellectual property laws governing design practices. More specifically, in the article, 'The Piracy Paradox', Raustiala and Sprigman (2006) contend that the fashion industry presents a unique exception to the widespread assumption that the copying of literary and artistic works stifles competition. They have observed that in the world of fashion and apparel, the pervasiveness of design copying (as opposed to the copying of designer trademarks) spurs rather than stifles innovation, and may even be beneficial for designers in their production of creative content. In their view, 'competition, innovation, and investment [in fashion] remain [paradoxically] vibrant' (2006: 1689). The so-called piracy paradox characteristic of the fashion industry challenges the standard theory of intellectual property rights, which predicts that copying presents disincentives for creativity and innovation in any given industry. As they assert, this paradox is, in large part, explained by the fact that the drive for innovation in apparel design relies on the following characteristics of the fashion economy: (1) the timely and ongoing introduction of new fashion trends via practices of design copying, as well as (2) the role that fashion goods play as signifiers of class position, social status and market access for fashion producers and consumers.

Though their analysis insightfully points to the relational dynamics and contradictions inherent in the notions of creativity and newness, I suggest that their analysis overlooks the social impacts of design copying upon participants other than designers within the wider political economy of fast fashion. The pervasiveness of design copying among competing bosses in Guangzhou, for example, further accelerates the turnover of fashion commodities in the industry and intensifies wider pressures of market competition and dwindling profits.

[3]In her book, Anna Tsing (2005) describes 'friction' as the tensions and contradictions that emerge through moments of cultural misunderstanding and awkward engagement. Capitalist exchanges operate through universal categories, which, as Tsing highlights, remain localised and contested. Creativity, within the realm of fast fashion, may be seen as one of these universal categories. Once put into action, its essential definition becomes blurred and ambiguous.

[4]As Moon (2017) writes, 'Fast-fashion reflects the highly volatile and precarious nature of global fashion markets – consumers, with finicky tastes that quickly shift and change, now demand a wider variety of design trends, at cheaper prices.'

Design copying signals both a trend's dual creative and destructive potential, which, in many ways, mirrors what Joseph Schumpeter describes (1975) as creative destruction. Though a particular design requires copying in order to become a trend, *too much* copying by market competitors signals its eventual death (Benjamin 1968; Taussig 2012; Chumley 2016). The ongoing cycles and pressures of the market compel many migrant entrepreneurs, in turn, to aspire to engage in more high-end, 'creative' endeavours in order to extract themselves from the fast turnover of market trends characteristic of fast fashion. They aspire to join the coveted ranks of the privileged 'creative classes' in the hopes of scaling up the fashion supply chains and owning unique brands and labels. Therefore, the key engine of market activity, as I argue, is the unyielding competition among participants for access to market niches and spaces where they are most profitable. Once they have established a foothold in the fashion market, migrant entrepreneurs are then concerned with maintaining market access, that is, sustaining their risky business endeavours in light of the ongoing turnover of commodities, marketspaces and capital.

Flipping spaces: spatialising the cycles of fast fashion as a rent-seeking activity

The class-based divisions among competing bosses are reflected in the spatial organisation of Guangzhou's wholesale markets. These divisions intersect with competing notions and discourses of creativity among market participants. Tightly cramped, informal stalls occupy the first four levels of the building. These stalls sell clothing and accessories to intermediary buyers primarily from lower-tiered cities in China and in export hubs throughout Southeast Asia, including Taiwan, Malaysia, Singapore, Vietnam and Indonesia. Turnover of fashion trends cycles most rapidly along the lower floors of the market, primarily because the goods sold here are offered at lower prices and at lower quantities per order.

In order to keep up with the incessant movement of goods in and out of the building, the majority of migrant entrepreneurs on the lower market levels experience constant pressures to produce new clothing. In fact, new styles are introduced nearly every week. The styles sold on the lower floors are generally casual junior wear featuring brightly coloured prints, flowery dresses, bold tops, eye-catching accessories and message T-shirts. These stalls attract the most shoppers, which are visibly evidenced by the crowds of onlookers who flood the hallways. Visitors come to the market in order to buy garments at extremely low volumes (at most 10–20 pieces per order), since many intermediary brokers frequent the market at least several times per season. The lower market floors offer the trendiest fashions at the lowest price points, which generally range from 20–100 RMB (3–15 USD) per piece.

The cramped stalls, overcrowded hallways and makeshift organisation of the lower floors stand in sharp contrast to the upper floors of the building, which consist of larger, more formalised boutiques that look as if they are set up as offices and showrooms rather than the informal stalls of the lower floors. The clothing and accessories that are sold here often feature subdued colours, boxy and angular styles and solids (rather than prints). These items are usually more expensive, appealing to shoppers who prefer more formal, professional looks. Because of the higher price points, fewer shoppers roam the upper levels. Young female sellers are often seen packaging massive bundles of clothing in bulk as they prepare to ship these parcels to overseas customers. The volume of their orders is usually larger, ranging from a few hundred to a thousand pieces per order. Since fewer clients visit the upper floors, the pace of work life along the upper floors of the market is much slower and calmer than that of the lower floors.

Meanwhile, the timing of fashion seasons, along with their cyclical flows of commodities and capital in and out of the market floors, open up opportunities for building managers to inflate rent and management fees. Rents in the wholesale market have risen over the past few years due to inflationary pressures within the city's real estate market, compounded by price fluctuations in the global commodities market for cotton and other raw materials. The majority of stalls that occupy the lower levels of the wholesale market are frequently replaced by new, incoming entrepreneurs every 10–12 months. Building managers have a personal interest in maintaining the ongoing turnover of new lessees, since newcomers are easier to extort cash fees and other payments from. More established, long-term occupants tend to maintain close ties to more powerful building administrators, so they are more difficult to bribe.

Stall owners that I have spoken with often complain about how difficult it is to maintain their businesses there because of the market's exorbitant rent. A compact 5 × 7 feet stall on the first four levels of the market costs over 10,000 RMB a month, five times the average monthly income of a Guangzhou resident. Spacious offices on the fifth through ninth floors cost as much as 150,000 RMB a month, plus 20,000 RMB in monthly management fees. After contracts are renewed every three to five years, rents continue to rise despite the steep downturn in business activity since the global economic slowdown beginning in 2008. As a consequence, the turnover rate of new businesses entering this market and failed businesses exiting through its revolving door remains high, so much so that the average stall lasts only 10–12 months. The high turnover of migrant entrepreneurs, stall spaces, fashion commodities and money in and out of the market premises merely exacerbates the rising costs of renting commercial spaces there.

The spatial, temporal and bureaucratic organisation of the management team within the building also reflects the extractive and policing activities that are part and parcel of the everyday order of conducting business there. Each of the nine floors of the market is supervised by a manager (usually a person who is fluent in the Cantonese local dialect) who is responsible for leasing market stalls and boutiques to renters. Every supervisor leads a team of four to five assistants, who help carry out tasks assigned by their boss. Floor-level supervisors usually make daily rounds along the hallways in order to confirm that certain security measures, fire safety codes and intellectual property laws are enforced and followed by visitors, tenants and employees. Meanwhile, their assistants check for legitimate *hukou* identification and valid business licences on a weekly basis among the bosses and their employees in order to confirm that no one working inside the building is an undocumented migrant. Anyone caught without proper IDs and licences would face arrest and immediate closure of their business.

The managers' regulatory activities within the building are timed according to the yearly cycles of fast fashion, which open up lucrative opportunities for monetary extractions from their renters. During the months of August and September leading up to Guangzhou's famous trade show, the Canton Fair, most international clients filter through Guangzhou in search of the newest fall trends. This September trade show marks the beginning of the fall season, coinciding with Fashion Week in New York,

Paris and London. Many new stalls and boutiques pop up in the wholesale markets, while factories that handle garments for direct export to Euro-America receive production orders in July in preparation for the following spring collection. The most intensive and frequent policing work is conducted at this time in order to regulate the heavy traffic of visitors and goods that pass through the market floors.

The weeks following the annual Chinese New Year mark an influx of new renters and business operations within the building. During this time, renters along the market floors are each expected to provide a *hongbao*, or lucky money placed in a red envelope (or 5–20 RMB), to every building manager. These gifts act as symbolic gestures to sustain relationships of reciprocity (*guanxi*) between tenants and building managers in case special favours, including exceptions to intellectual property laws, have to be curried in the future. March and April mark the beginning of the spring season, when regulation and fee collection by building management are also frequent, while the period from June through August, a term known locally as *dam gui* (off-season), is characterised as the slowest business period in the year. At this time, building managers clear out the spaces once occupied by former tenants while they solicit and interview potential new clients. Unlike the months of February and early September during which most of the merchandise is cleared out at discounted rates (a process referred to as *qing huo*), the months of June through August mark the slowest business period for manufacturers and wholesalers in the yearly fashion calendar. During this time, business in the markets slows down dramatically, and many garment factories temporarily close, forcing migrants to retreat to their home villages.

Building managers exploit the temporal gaps in the turnover of the fashion season by regulating the inflows and outflows of tenants and marketspaces. Before new tenants set up their businesses in the building, the managers require these newcomers to renovate their rental spaces regardless of the costs. Current tenants must also renovate their stalls and boutiques regularly in order to bring a certain sense of 'newness' to their goods. During the summer off-season, the Xi Fang Hang market temporarily closes once a year, so that all tenants can renovate their interior spaces. Throughout these summer months, building managers attempt to solicit tenants by guiding them through the vacant spaces and discussing the market's rental terms. The turnover of tenants and rental spaces allows managers to raise the costs of leasing there. A long-time wholesaler of garment accessories in the building once remarked, 'They [the building managers] don't care whether you can afford it [the rent increases] or not, they'll just raise the rent. If you can't pay, then you'll have to leave!'

In fact, a construction company owned by a wealthy Guangzhou-based real estate developer occupies a large office space on the ninth floor of Xi Fang Hang, indicating the regularity of speculative remodelling that is required by the building management. The strategic location of this construction office within the building has led market sellers and visitors to speculate that some business managers share a portion of their income from rent with other so-called insiders through various forms of kickbacks. For instance, Helen, a young wholesaler from Dongbei, whose showroom occupies the ninth floor, has informed me that any building repair must be handled by the building management for a fee. She states, 'If they change a light or even hammer a nail on the wall, managers would charge you 300 RMB for the job.' Additionally, a factory owner who handles the production of many garments sold at Xi Fang Hang once stated,

'Many of my clients complain to me how difficult it is to do business there, because the rent's too expensive. Do you think that just by remodelling they'll really upgrade [the market]? They [the management] will just fix a light fixture here or nail something there and they'll charge you double the rent for it!' Other shoppers speculate that undercover shoppers would regularly scope the markets to observe which stalls attract the most clients. If management sees that a stall owner's business succeeds, then management fees will increase accordingly.

The influence and authority that building managers maintain foster intricate webs of profitable and cushy patron–client relationships among supervisors, clients and other powerful bosses. Oftentimes, building administrators expect monetary kickbacks whenever they assist in facilitating business mergers (usually through introductions among personal friends and existing tenants within the building), terminate long-term leases among tenants before their contracts expire, and overlook certain exceptions to legal codes or business procedures such as allowing certain counterfeit items to be sold upon market premises or permitting some bosses to operate without proper licenses and identification papers.

Furthermore, managers usually allow a number of informal and secretive businesses to occupy the upper levels of the wholesale market in exchange for compensation fees or kickbacks. These ventures are usually run by long-standing insiders of Guangzhou's garment industry who act as intermediary brokers between building managers and newly arrived tenants who are interested in expanding their business. They covertly mediate disputes among competing bosses, arrange available stall spaces and boutiques for potential clients, facilitate business alliances and gather market forecasting details. Outside observers suspect that the building management is increasingly being monopolised by a small group of established entrepreneurs who have run very successful businesses since the early inception of this wholesale market in the 1990s. According to some market participants, these Guangzhou-based entrepreneurs have formed an informal business association, whereby they set industry-wide prices on fabric, finished garments and rental stalls. Regardless of the veracity of these observations, the rumours surrounding the ongoing spatial transformations accentuate the growing sense of inequality and inaccessibility among struggling small-scale entrepreneurs located on the lower floors of the building relative to the more established bosses. The patron–client networks among wealthy bosses, building managers and tenants are facilitated and sustained by an exchange of fees and kickbacks.

Flipping time: the 'just-in-time' delivery of fast fashion

In light of the spatial turnover of money and commodities, small-scale entrepreneurs and other informal workers labouring on the lower floors of the market struggle to keep pace with demanding production schedules and rising costs of rent while they search for novel ways of making fast money. Their timely rhythms attest to the dynamic circulation of fast fashion production and design, which straddle ambiguously between creativity and copying (Thrift 2006). Wholesalers emphasise the speed at which clothes must be translated from the pictorial image to the actual finished garments. The entire process, starting from placing an order with the local manufacturer, through choosing the appropriate fabrics and accessories, then mass manufacturing, to final assembly in packages, involves only about two to three days' turnaround.

Aided by modern technologies including the Internet, mobile phones, iPhones and iPads, domestic and transnational wholesalers from Xi Fang Hang and other markets bring selected images with them as they scour the fabric market in Guangzhou's garment district in order to search for the most appropriate fabrics, accessories and raw materials. Agents deliver these materials to garment factories and workshops behind the fabric market. These factories are often referred to as *jiagongchang*, or assembly factories (Chu 2016). The term *jiagongchang* or assembly sites refers to factories that specifically provide the human labour necessary in garment manufacture and assembly at a scale usually ranging from 100–2000 pieces per order. Specialised labour is divided among these production sites, because certain types of fabric require particular labour techniques and machines in the process of garment manufacture. For example, certain *jiagongchang* only specialise in particular kinds of fabrics such as denim, chiffon or synthetic silks, since their production requires specific machines and human skill. These production sites rely primarily on temporary work provided by the city's precarious migrant population, whose labour is divided along the garment production chain in which their factories specialise. For instance, *da ban gong* or sample-making factories create paper patterns and produce the necessary garment samples before they are sent to larger factories for large-scale manufacture.

Because of the tight and unforgiving cycles of payment and debt, the creation and delivery of new styles constantly pose new risks of monetary loss. For agents and stall owners, the work of choosing garment samples almost always entails a certain degree of risk, because there is no guarantee that a certain style will sell. In fact, Sophie, a wholesaler in the Xi Fang Hang market, once explained to me that she tends to choose simpler styles for her clients. For her, styles that are too complicated or too flashy are too risky, so they are 'not worth making'. Leftover inventory that fails to sell in time during the appropriate fashion season is stored in warehouses before it is cleared at discounted prices. Unsold goods that impede the continuous flow of commodities and capital thus cut into potential investment opportunities of wholesalers. Indeed, one bad investment decision at any period of time may set off a ripple effect of debt for other market participants along the supply chain. Meanwhile, debts may quickly accumulate, potentially leading Sophie and other small-scale entrepreneurs down a spiral of delinquency, debt and bankruptcy.

Cycles of debt and bankruptcy: the social costs of design copying

Despite the enormous risks entailed in running a stall at Xi Fang Hang, migrant entrepreneurs attempt to stake a claim in this market by pooling their family's resources in the hopes of striking it rich while enjoying the independence that comes with being their own bosses. For example, Ling, a savvy 26-year-old woman, recently closed down her 5 × 7-feet stall after running her business for only about two years based on savings that she had pooled from her family in nearby Foshan. When her wholesale business for women's beach dresses failed, she decided to take a step back from the pressures of running a stall there so that she could brainstorm her next business endeavour. Ultimately, she dreamed of resuming her business in this market so that she could try her luck again.

With her eyes beaming, she exclaimed, 'Just before the 2008 market crash, some bosses (*laoban*) were making as much as 10,000 RMB (2000 USD) a day! If you can make it there, you can make volumes of money. The returns are huge … '

As Ling observed, the rise of rent, coupled with the widespread prevalence of copying in Xi Fang Hang, undercut the stability and vibrancy of market relations as a whole. She explained that the costs of renting stalls had nearly doubled over the past two or three years, making her former business impossible to sustain. Since the global economic downturn in 2008, fewer foreign clients passed through the front doors of Guangzhou's wholesale markets. The rising costs of cotton and other raw materials since 2010 also thwarted sellers' abilities to provide desirable garments of top quality. As a means of evading these economic risks, numerous sellers in the highly competitive Xi Fang Hang market resorted to copying competitors' designs (with minimal to no modification) in order to stay financially afloat. With limited unique styles to choose from, clients were increasingly turning to wholesale outlets online rather than visiting the market. As Ling noted, extensive copying without design modifications was more common when business declined. She admitted that design copying, where identical garments were sold by competing wholesalers, was a pervasive practice, and speculated that copying at a mass-scale would eventually hurt the larger group of competing business owners. In her view, copying intensified the competitive atmosphere among wholesalers, while clients were offered fewer choices of lower quality.

When I asked Ling whether she had personally experienced someone copying from her, she recounted a time when a personal friend of hers, a wealthy local boss who operated a boutique in one of the upper floors of the market, introduced Ling to a younger cousin of hers. The boss asked Ling to show this younger relative the ropes of the fashion trade. Ling agreed, and added this young woman as her employee. Over the course of six months, the young woman learned most, if not all, of Ling's business secrets, including her aesthetic style, design strategies and business contacts, and opened a competing stall directly next to Ling's using her relative's money. To Ling's dismay, her stall mirrored most, if not all, of Ling's garment styles and fashion aesthetic, including the interior decorations of her stall. When Ling confronted the woman and the wealthy boss, they simply claimed that their 'look' was uniquely original. Since the young woman claimed to have studied fashion design before, her assertion of originality seemed more credible to other wholesalers and clients at the time. With less capital and fewer resources at hand, Ling conceded, 'What can you do? Business is business. By the time someone copies you the styles would have already changed anyways.'

Another migrant entrepreneur, Edwin, a former wholesaler in Xi Fang Hang, admitted to having relied on design copying to jumpstart his business, since design copying was pervasive there. He explained that once business owners became privy to a certain style or design that sold well, competitors would quickly copy the exact design within two to three days. They would either directly copy an entire look with minor modifications or simply purchase a garment piece from a competitor and retag it as their own. By then, one could see that several store-owners had already sold that very same design. Migrant entrepreneurs must then constantly create new styles in order to remain competitive. As Edwin emphasised, the fact that a competitor copied his design implied that the business owner had achieved a level of success and admiration from her competitors. His statement seemed to suggest that, contrary to Ling's opinion, copying was advantageous to wholesalers because, in many ways, the practice of design copying signalled public recognition. In his view, success as a wholesaler secured financial freedom, while also eliciting acceptance and admiration from others.

Edwin further reasoned that the preponderance of copying among local markets bore witness to the fact that the wholesale niche should facilitate a slow, reflective response to the market. The volume of new fashions that rotated in and out of the wholesale markets moved too quickly to nurture and facilitate the necessary time and creative space for sellers to reflect upon the changed market and respond accordingly with new designs. Even retailers, the clients of the wholesalers that I discuss here, often complained about neighbouring competitors who attempted to copy their designs by choosing the same merchandise to sell. I once overheard a young seller in a retail market complaining about her neighbour in the next stall. She said, 'Now if you compare her clothes with mine, what differences are there? She had explicitly promised me to not worry because she wouldn't pick up *my* style and taste.' Her sympathetic friend expressed her support for the distressed woman by saying, 'Yes, the clothes that you picked up depend on your discerning eye and *feel* for fashion', as if creativity was endowed as a talent or skill cultivated by years of learning and experience. Their exchange unveiled the contentious discourse around copying and the painstaking efforts among industry participants in claiming and authenticating one's creativity as the purveyor of fashion.

Conclusion

The everyday rhythms of exchange within Guangzhou's fashion markets thus complicate Raustiala and Sprigman's singular focus on design copying as the key driver of innovation and creative content. In Guangzhou's fast fashion sector, creativity operates as practices in boundary-making, which produce the uneven rhythms and spaces that link up with the industry's rapid turnover of trends. In marketspaces like Xi Fang Hang, fast fashion commodities act as what Star and Griesemer describe as 'boundary objects', which straddle between fashion and non-fashion, as well as original design and design copying. The categorical lines that distinguish creativity from design copying are thus often unclear. The blurring of such boundaries compels market participants to use competing definitions and practices of inventiveness and copying as regulatory functions over the quick and speculative turnover of marketspaces and fashion trends. Together, these contestations are what I describe as paradoxes of creativity. While building managers and wealthy entrepreneurs mobilise techniques of rent extraction, quality control and labour discipline under the guise of 'creativity', less established migrant entrepreneurs use design copying as a tool for market survival. Such contestations mask the class-based divisions among building managers, wealthy local bosses, and migrant entrepreneurs as they attempt to pass on market risks to other competitors in fast fashion's 'race to the bottom'.

Acknowledgements

This essay was written while I was a Postdoctoral Associate in the School of Industrial and Labor Relations (the ILR School) at Cornell University. I thank Teri Silvio, Lily Chumley and two anonymous readers at *Culture, Theory and Critique* for their generous and insightful comments. I have also benefitted from comments provided by Lisa Rofel, Melissa Caldwell, Gail Hershatter and

Jeremy Tai, who read early drafts of this paper while I was a graduate student at the University of California, Santa Cruz.

Disclosure statement

No potential conflict of interest was reported by the author.

Funding

Research for this project was made possible by the Global and Transregional Studies Platform (formerly known as the Center for Transregional Research Network CETREN) at the University of Göttingen in Germany.

References

Benjamin, W. 1968. 'Theses on the Philosophy of History'. In Hannah Arendt (ed), *Illuminations: Essays and Reflections by Walter Benjamin*. New York, NY: Random House, 253–64.

Chu, N. 2016. 'The Emergence of "Craft" and Migrant Entrepreneurship Across the Global Commodity Chains for Fast Fashion in Southern China'. *The Journal of Modern Craft* 9:2, 193–213.

Chumley, L. 2016. *Creativity Class: Art School and Culture Work in Postsocialist China*. Princeton, NJ: Princeton University Press.

Coombe, R. 1998. *The Cultural Life of Intellectual Properties: Authorship, Appropriation, and the Law*. Durham, NC: Duke University Press.

English, B. 2013. *A Cultural History of Fashion in the 20th and 21st Centuries: From Catwalk to Sidewalk*. London: Bloomsberg.

Florida, R. 2002. *The Rise of the Creative Class: And How It's Transforming Work, Leisure, Community, and Everyday Life*. New York, NY: Basic Books.

Florida, R. 2005. *Cities and the Creative Class*. New York, NY: Routledge.

Florida, R. 2011. *The Rise of the Creative Class: Revisited*. New York, NY: Basic Books.

Harvey, D. 2001. *Spaces of Capital: Towards a Critical Geography*. New York, NY: Routledge.

Horning, R. 2011. 'The Accidental Brioleurs.' n+1, June. Available online at https://nplusonemag.com/online-only/online-only/the-accidental-bricoleurs/.

Lin, Y. 2011. *Fake Stuff: China and the Rise of Counterfeit Goods*. Milton Park: Taylor & Francis.

Mason, M. 2008. *The Pirate's Dilemma: How Youth Culture is Reinventing Capitalism*. New York, NY: Free Press.

Moon, C. 2014. 'The Secret World of Fast Fashion'. *Pacific Standard*, March. Available online at https://psmag.com/economics/secret-world-slow-road-korea-los-angeles-behind-fast-fashion-73956.

Moon, C. 2017. 'To Dwell in Seams'. *Anthropology News*, September. Available online at http://www.anthropology-news.org/index.php/2017/09/08/to-dwell-in-seams/.

Nakassis, C. 2013. 'Citation and Citationality'. *Signs and Society* 1:1, 51–77.

Pang, L. 2012. *Creativity and Its Discontents: China's Creative Industries and Intellectual Property Offenses*. Durham, NC: Duke University Press.

Park, S. 2012. 'Stitching the Fabric of Family: Time, Work, and Intimacy in Seoul's Tongdaemun Market'. *The Journal of Korean Studies* 17:2, 383–406.

Raustiala, K. and Sprigman, C. 2006. 'The Piracy Paradox: Innovation and Intellectual Property in Fashion Design'. *Virginia Law Review* 92:8, 1687–777.

Schumpeter, J. 1975. *Capitalism, Socialism, and Democracy*. New York, NY: Harper Publishing.

Starr, S.L. and Griesemer, J. R. 1989. 'Institutional Ecology, "Translations" and Boundary Objects: Amateurs and Professionals in Berkeley's Museum of Vertebrate Zoology, 1907–39'. *Social Studies of Science* 19:3, 387–420.

Taussig, M. 2012. *Beauty and the Beast*. Chicago, IL: University of Chicago Press.

Thomas, K. 2012. 'Intellectual Property Law and the Ethics of Imitation in Guatemala'. *Anthropological Quarterly* 85:3, 785–815.

Thomas, K. 2016. *Regulating Style: Intellectual Property Law and the Business of Fashion in Guatemala*. Berkeley, CA: University of California Press.

Thrift, Nigel. 2006. 'Space'. *Theory, Culture, and Society* 23:2-3, 139–46.

Tsing, A. 2005. *Friction: An Ethnography of Global Connection*. Princeton, NJ: Princeton University Press.

Vann, E. 2006. 'The Limits of Authenticity in Vietnamese Consumer Markets'. *American Anthropologist* 108:2, 286–96.

Index

Note: Page numbers in *italics* refer to figures.

Index

Note: Page numbers in *italics* refer to figures.